Contents

Popular progression pathways

General qualification	Vocationally related qualification	Applied qualification
Undergraduate Degree	BTEC Higher National	Foundation Degree
GCE AS and A level	BTEC National	Advanced Diploma
GCSE	BTEC First	Higher (L2) and Foundation (L1) Diplomas

Your BTEC First course
Early days

Every year many new learners start BTEC Level 2 First courses, enjoy the challenge and successfully achieve their award. Some do this the easy way; others make it harder for themselves.

Everyone will have different feelings when they start their course.

Case study: Thinking positively

Most learners are a little nervous about starting a new course. Samantha is no exception. She went to an induction day just before the summer holidays. During this induction day, Samantha met other learners who will be starting the BTEC First in Sport with her. She also had a taste for what she would be doing in her lessons. There would be many practical activities, and she would have the chance to learn about the human body and how it responds to exercise. She finds this really interesting.

Now the summer holidays are over, Samantha is starting to worry about how she will do on the course. Samantha needs to try to think positively, as she thinks she will enjoy the course and it is something that she has been looking forward to for some time.

Rather than worry and think negative thoughts, such as 'what if all the other students are better at sports than me', Samantha should turn these into positive thoughts. She thinks, 'I can really improve my techniques if I play against people who are better than me, but I am bound to be better than some people at some sports – especially swimming as that is my favourite sport'.

Samantha also has doubts about the coursework. 'The practical activities about the human body sound really great, but what if I find them too difficult?' Samantha turns this into a positive thought, telling herself, 'the whole point of doing a course like this is to learn new skills and techniques'.

About your course

What do you know already?

If someone asks you about your course, could you give a short, accurate description? If you can, you have a good understanding of what your course is about. This has several benefits.

Four benefits of understanding your course

1. You will be better prepared and organised.

2. You can make links between the course and the world around you.

3. You can check how your personal interests and hobbies relate to the course.

4. You will be alert to information that relates to topics you are studying, whether it's from conversations with family and friends, watching television or at a part-time job.

Read any information you have been given by your centre. You can also check the Edexcel website for further details – go to www.edexcel.com.

Interest/hobby	How this relates to my studies

What else do you need to know?

Five facts you should find out about your course

1. The type of BTEC qualification you are studying.

2. How many credits your qualification is worth.

3. The number of mandatory units you will study and what they cover.

4. How many credits the mandatory units are worth.

5. The number of optional units you need to study in total and the options available in your centre.

Case study: What will I study?

Karl is 14 years old and is about to start his BTEC First Diploma in Sport, which he will complete in two years' time. He will also be taking several GCSEs including maths, English and double science. Karl wants to eventually have a career in the sports industry, so is hoping to progress to the BTEC National in Sport. He hopes to take this course either at college or in his school sixth form.

Sarah has completed her GCSEs, but did not do as well as she had hoped. Her school did not offer BTECs, so she is starting

her BTEC Diploma in Sport at a local college. Her course will only take her one year to complete, as she will be studying for this qualification on a full-time basis and she will not be taking any other GCSEs at the same time.

Both Karl and Sarah are studying for the same course, but over different periods of time. At the end of the course, if they are successful they will both have the equivalent of four GCSEs and also have the potential of studying for a BTEC National in Sport.

BTEC FACT

BTEC First Certificate = 15 credits

BTEC First Extended Certificate = 30 credits

BTEC First Diploma = 60 credits

Generally, the more credits there are, the longer it takes to study for the qualification.

TRY THIS

Find out which optional units your centre offers. To check the topics covered in each unit go to www. pearsonhotlinks.co.uk, insert the express code 5681S and click on the link for this page.

TOP TIPS

If you have a choice of optional units in your centre and are struggling to decide, talk through your ideas with your tutor.

Activity: How well do you know your course?

Complete this activity to check that you know the main facts. Compare your answers with a friend. You should have similar answers except where you make personal choices, such as about optional units. Your tutor can help you complete number 9.

1 The correct title of the BTEC award I am studying is:

2 The length of time it will take me to complete my award is:

3 The number of mandatory units I have to study is:

4 The titles of my mandatory units, and their credit values, are:

5 The main topics I will learn in each mandatory unit include:

Mandatory unit	Main topics

6 The number of credits I need to achieve by studying optional units is:

7 The titles of my optional units, and their credit values, are:

8 The main topics I will learn in each optional unit include:

Optional unit	Main topics

9 Other important aspects of my course are:

_____

_____

_____

_____

10 After I have achieved my BTEC First, my options include:

_____

_____

_____

_____

_____

Introduction to the sport sector

A BTEC Level 2 First in Sport is one of the most popular BTEC courses. There are many reasons why this course is in such demand, and you will experience some of these at first hand during next year or so.

The BTEC Level 2 First in Sport is a vocational qualification that will help prepare you for a huge range of careers. You may be thinking of pursuing a career either as an elite sports performer or as a coach. At present there are around 1.2 million coaches in Britain.

You may be considering joining the health and fitness industry as an exercise professional. This job requires you to supervise and instruct people who are taking part in exercise classes or exercise sessions. Research demonstrates a clear link between an active lifestyle and good health. As a result, the health and fitness industry has grown substantially over the last ten years, and it will probably continue to grow. There is a demand for exercise professionals, and there are good employment opportunities.

Alternatively, you may feel that working in outdoor adventure is for you. The outdoors sector is growing. This means that there is a demand for outdoor education professionals, and again there are good employment opportunities.

In your BTEC First in Sport you will be studying a wide range of units. All relate to sport. You will learn about your body and how it responds to exercise. This will help you to understand how and why your body responds to training. It will also help you understand your own or other people's training programmes.

You will also study risk assessment and legislation related to sport, including the Health and Safety at Work Act. This will help you ensure your training or coaching sessions are safe for all participants. You will also learn how to deal with injuries and illnesses associated with taking part in sports.

There are also several specialist units that you will study. Each of these units is designed to help you gain a better understanding of:

- the body
- the mind
- diet
- practical skills
- fitness
- training methods.

Knowledge of these areas can have a huge impact on sports performance. In addition, you will gain a good understanding of how the sports industry can influence sports performance and participation.

Skills you need for sport

For virtually all careers in the sport and leisure industry, you will need:
- good communication skills
- good interpersonal skills
- the ability to work well as a member of a team
- the ability to lead a team
- the ability to manage your time effectively

TOP TIPS

Having a positive can-do attitude to life is very important in sport.

Studying for the BTEC First in Sport allows you to practise all these skills utilising different styles of learning. You will encounter various methods to assess your understanding and knowledge of the different subject areas.

More about BTEC Level 2 Firsts

What is different about a BTEC Level 2 First?

How you learn

Expect to be 'hands-on'. BTEC Level 2 Firsts are practical and focus on the skills and knowledge needed in the workplace. You will learn new things and learn how to apply your knowledge.

BTEC First learners are expected to take responsibility for their own learning and be keen and well-organised. You should enjoy having more freedom, while knowing you can still ask for help or support if you need it.

How you are assessed

Many BTEC First courses are completed in one year, but if you are taking GCSEs as well, you may be doing it over two years or more. You will be assessed by completing **assignments** written by your tutors. These are based on **learning outcomes** set by Edexcel. Each assignment will have a deadline.

Case study: Annabel's story

Annabel studied for GCSEs at school and she was predicted good grades. However, when it came to examination time, Annabel became very nervous. She started to get very stressed about sitting the exams. She didn't perform as well as she had hoped, and she ended up getting lower grades than had been predicted.

Annabel wanted to progress to A-level equivalent courses. To do this, she had the choice of resitting some of her GCSEs or taking a BTEC First in Sport. She found the BTEC in Sport course very interesting and, more importantly for Annabel, there were no exams. The entire course was assessed through coursework.

Even better, the coursework wasn't just writing essays. Annabel was assessed through different methods, including designing leaflets and posters, delivering PowerPoint presentations, and taking part in role-play exercises.

Annabel completed the BTEC First in Sport with distinction grades, and she went on to take a BTEC National in Sport. Again she did very well. She is now at university continuing her studies in sport.

Getting the most from your BTEC

Getting the most from your BTEC involves several skills, such as using your time effectively and working well with other people. Knowing yourself is also important.

Knowing yourself

How would you describe yourself? Make some notes here.

_____

_____

_____

_____

_____

_____

_____

_____

If you described yourself to someone else, would you be able to sum up your temperament and personality, identify your strengths and weaknesses and list your skills? If not, is it because you've never thought about it or because you honestly don't have a clue?

Learning about yourself is often called self-analysis. You may have already done personality tests or careers profiles. If not, there are many available online. However, the information you gain from these profiles is useless unless you can apply it to what you are doing.

Your personality

Everyone is different. For example, some people:

- like to plan in advance; others prefer to be spontaneous
- love being part of a group; others prefer one or two close friends
- enjoy being the life and soul of the party; others prefer to sit quietly, and feel uncomfortable at large social gatherings
- are imaginative and creative; others prefer to deal only with facts
- think carefully about all their options before making a decision; others follow their 'gut instincts' and often let their heart rule their head.

Activity: Moving out of your comfort zone

If you feel that you are becoming stuck in a rut, that you are doing the same things day in day out, why not have a go at this two-week challenge? It will help to get the most out of everyday life.

The challenge requires you to do something different at least once each day. It has to be something that takes you out of your comfort zone.

Here are some possible challenges:
- get out of bed an hour earlier than usual
- take part in a new sport
- start your assignment the day it is handed out
- complete your assignment well before the hand-in date.

You should aim to set challenges that are achievable, but which also make some difference to your current life and routine.

In the spaces below, list at least one challenge a day for the next two-week period.

Day 1

Day 2

Day 3

Day 4

Day 5

Day 6

Day 7

Day 8

Day 9

Day 10

Day 11

Day 12

Day 13

Day 14

By challenging yourself and completing these challenges, you will increase your self-belief and your confidence in what you can achieve.

TRY THIS

Imagine one of your friends is describing your best features. What would they say?

Personalities in the workplace

There's a mix of personalities in most workplaces. Some people prefer to work behind the scenes, such as many IT practitioners, who like to concentrate on tasks they enjoy doing. Others love high-profile jobs, where they may often be involved in high-pressure situations, such as paramedics and television presenters. Most people fall somewhere between these two extremes.

In any job there will be some aspects that are more appealing and interesting than others. If you have a part-time job you will already know this. The same thing applies to any course you take!

Your personality and your BTEC First course

Understanding your personality means you can identify which parts of your course you are likely to find easy and which more difficult. Working out the aspects you need to develop should be positive. You can also think about how your strengths and weaknesses may affect other people.

- Natural planners find it easier to schedule work for assignments.
- Extroverts like giving presentations and working with others but may overwhelm quieter team members.
- Introverts often prefer to work alone and may be excellent at researching information.

BTEC FACT

All BTEC First courses enable you to develop your personal, learning and thinking skills (**PLTS**), which will help you to meet new challenges more easily. (See page 87.)

Activity: What is your personality type?

1a) Identify your own personality type, either by referring to a personality test you have done recently or by going online and doing a reliable test. Go to www.pearsonhotlinks.co.uk, insert the express code 5681S and click on the link for this activity.

Print a summary of the completed test or write a brief description of the results for future reference.

b) Use this information to identify the tasks and personal characteristics that you find easy or difficult.

	Easy	Difficult
Being punctual		
Planning how to do a job		
Working neatly and accurately		
Being well organised		
Having good ideas		
Taking on new challenges		
Being observant		
Working with details		
Being patient		
Coping with criticism		
Dealing with customers		
Making decisions		
Keeping calm under stress		
Using your own initiative		

	Easy	Difficult
Researching facts carefully and accurately		
Solving problems		
Meeting deadlines		
Finding and correcting own errors		
Clearing up after yourself		
Helping other people		
Working as a member of a team		
Being sensitive to the needs of others		
Respecting other people's opinions		
Being tactful and discreet		
Being even-tempered		

2 Which thing from your 'difficult' list do you think you should work on improving first? Start by identifying the benefits you will gain. Then decide how to achieve your goal.

Your knowledge and skills

You already have a great deal of knowledge, as well as practical and personal skills gained at school, at home and at work (if you have a part-time job). Now you need to assess these to identify your strengths and weaknesses.

To do this accurately, try to identify evidence for your knowledge and skills. Obvious examples are:

- previous qualifications
- school reports
- occasions when you have demonstrated particular skills, such as communicating with customers or colleagues in a part-time job.

Part-time jobs give you knowledge and skills in a real work setting.

TOP TIPS

The more you understand your own personality, the easier it is to build on your strengths and compensate for your weaknesses.

Activity: Check your skills

1 Score yourself from 1 to 5 for each of the skills in the table below.

1 = I'm very good at this skill.

2 = I'm good but could improve this skill.

3 = This skill is only average and I know that I need to improve it.

4 = I'm weak at this skill and must work hard to improve it.

5 = I've never had the chance to develop this skill.

Enter the score in the column headed 'Score A' and add today's date.

2 Look back at the units and topics you will be studying for your course – you entered them into the chart on pages 9–10. Use this to identify any additional skills that you know are important for your course and add them to the table. Then score yourself for these skills, too.

3 Identify the main skills you will need in order to be successful in your chosen career, and highlight them in the table.

Go back and score yourself against each skill after three, six and nine months. That way you can monitor your progress and check where you need to take action to develop the most important skills you will need.

English and communication skills	Score A	Score B (after three months)	Score C (after six months)	Score D (after nine months)
Test dates:				
Reading and understanding different types of texts and information				
Speaking to other people face to face				
Speaking clearly on the telephone				
Listening carefully				
Writing clearly and concisely				
Presenting information in a logical order				
Summarising information				
Using correct punctuation and spelling				
Joining in a group discussion				
Expressing your own ideas and opinions appropriately				
Persuading other people to do something				
Making an oral presentation and presenting ideas clearly				

ICT skills	Score A	Score B (after three months)	Score C (after six months)	Score D (after nine months)
Test dates:				
Using ICT equipment correctly and safely				
Using a range of software				
Accurate keyboarding				
Proofreading				
Using the internet to find and select appropriate information				
Using ICT equipment to communicate and exchange information				
Producing professional documents which include tables and graphics				
Creating and interpreting spreadsheets				
Using PowerPoint				

Maths and numeracy skills	Score A	Score B (after three months)	Score C (after six months)	Score D (after nine months)
Test dates:				
Carrying out calculations (eg money, time, measurements etc) in a work-related situation				
Estimating amounts				
Understanding and interpreting data in tables, graphs, diagrams and charts				
Comparing prices and identifying best value for money				
Solving routine and non-routine work-related numerical problems				

Activity: Different ways of learning

Many people taking a BTEC First in Sport like to learn through taking part in a physical activity. Do you find that you:

- enjoy sport, exercise and other physical activities?
- like to think out issues, ideas and problems while exercising?
- like to make models or complete jigsaws?
- use large hand gestures and other types of body language to communicate?
- can't sit still for long and often fidget?
- learn best when you are involved or active?
- use movement to help recall information?

If you find you agree with some of the statements, you may find that these tips help you get the most out of your study:

Physically touch objects as you learn about them

In anatomy lessons, for example, ask if you may touch any models of the skeleton and joints. Move the joints around to help you to learn about their function and characteristics.

Design your own flashcards

This will help you to remember information because you can touch and move the cards around. For example, when learning about sports nutrition, write carbohydrates on a large piece of paper and then draw pictures of foods that contain lots of carbohydrates.

Use role playing

This is where you 'act out' an event, either by yourself or with a friend. For example, when you are learning how to deal with an injury, design cards to show each of the injuries you need to know about. Then role-play in pairs. One of you selects a card and has to pretend to have the injury listed on the card, and the other has to guess what the injury is and treat it accordingly.

Draw diagrams

These are a good way to record key points. Use big sheets of paper and large colour pens to get more from the drawing. For example, you might draw a mind map to show the different risks and hazards associated with a specific sport or activity.

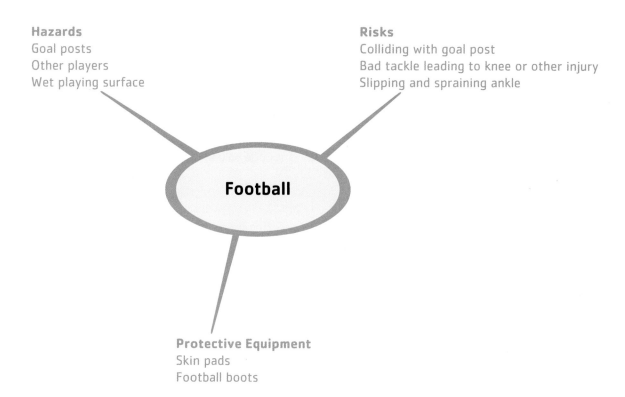

Hazards
Goal posts
Other players
Wet playing surface

Risks
Colliding with goal post
Bad tackle leading to knee or other injury
Slipping and spraining ankle

Football

Protective Equipment
Skin pads
Football boots

Have a go at drawing a mind map about a subject of your choice. For example, you might draw a mind map about how the body responds to exercise.

Managing your time

Some people are brilliant at managing their time. They do everything they need to and have time left over for activities they enjoy. Other people complain that they don't know where the time goes.

Which are you? If you need help to manage your time – and most people do – you will find help here.

Why time management is important

- It means you stay in control, get less stressed and don't skip important tasks.
- Some weeks will be peaceful, others will be hectic.
- The amount of homework and assignments you have to do will vary.
- As deadlines approach, time always seems to go faster.
- Some work will need to be done quickly, maybe for the next lesson; other tasks may need to be done over several days or weeks. This needs careful planning.
- You may have several assignments or tasks to complete in a short space of time.
- You want to have a social life.

Avoiding time–wasting

We can all plan to do work, and then find our plans go wrong. There may be several reasons for this. How many of the following do *you* do?

	Top time-wasting activities
1	Allowing (or encouraging) people to interrupt you.
2	Not having the information, handouts or textbook you need because you've lost them or lent them to someone else.
3	Chatting to people, making calls or sending texts when you should be working.
4	Getting distracted because you simply must keep checking out MySpace, Facebook or emails.
5	Putting off jobs until they are a total nightmare, then panicking.
6	Daydreaming.
7	Making a mess of something so you have to start all over again.

Case study: Avoid falling behind in your coursework

Anita was looking forward to starting her BTEC First in Sport, and she did well in her first term. All her assignments were handed in on time and she was getting some good grades.

However, during her second term, Anita became friends with a new group of girls. She went out nearly every night rather than do her homework. Eventually she stopped completing and handing in her assignments. Anita started to pretend that she was ill, so that she didn't have to go into school. She knew her tutors would be asking for assignment work to be handed in. She eventually got so far behind with her work that she didn't think she would complete the course.

Her tutor called a meeting with Anita and her parents. At the meeting Anita was in tears, saying she had so much work to do that she didn't know where to start. Her tutor then sat down with her, and they devised an action plan of how Anita could make a start on the mountain of backed-up work.

Each day, Anita has to research or answer one task from her outstanding assignments. One day a week counts as a rest day, during which Anita does not have to do any school work. Anita's parents have been asked to help ensure Anita completes her action plan. She is only allowed out to see her friends once that day's task has been completed.

Anita now feels much happier. It has taken a few months, but she is back on track and getting good grades for her work.

It is always a good idea to keep a diary of your assignments. You can record when assignments are issued, your progress on individual tasks, and when you handed in the assignments. This will help you be organised and be in control of your study time.

If you start to feel that you are unable to keep on top of the workload, talk to your tutor, your school or college librarian, or your parents or guardians. They can advise you and get you the right support. This will help you avoid the situation of having to catch up with a backlog of assignments that have accumulated over several weeks. Remember, it is never too late to seek help to get you back on track.

Planning and getting organised

The first step in managing your time is to plan ahead and be well organised. Some people are naturally good at this. They think ahead, write down their commitments in a diary or planner, and store their notes and handouts neatly and carefully so they can find them quickly.

How good are your working habits?

Improving your planning and organisational skills

1. Use a diary or planner to schedule working times into your weekdays and weekends.

2. Have a place for everything and everything in its place.

3. Be strict with yourself when you start work. If you aren't really in the mood, set a shorter time limit and give yourself a reward when the time is up.

4. Keep a diary in which you write down exactly what work you have to do.

5. Divide up long or complex tasks into manageable chunks and put each 'chunk' in your diary with a deadline of its own.

6. Write a 'to do' list if you have several different tasks. Tick them off as you go.

7. Always allow more time than you think you need for a task.

Talking to friends can take up a lot of time.

TRY THIS

Analyse your average day.

How many hours do you spend sleeping, eating, travelling, attending school or college, working, and taking part in leisure activities?

How much time is left for homework and assignments?

Case study: Avoiding time-wasters

Daniel is studying for a BTEC First in Sport qualification. During the first term of the course, Daniel was doing very well. His homework was competed on time, and he was achieving well in his assignments.

However this changed when Mike joined the school. Mike has become firm friends with Daniel. Mike spends more time chatting to Daniel in lessons than working, which means neither Daniel nor Mike are completing the work set by the tutor.

During lesson time set aside for assignment work, Mike distracts Daniel. When they are carrying out research on the internet, Mike encourages Daniel to surf websites that are not relevant to the set tasks.

Daniel is now falling behind with his work. His homework is rushed and his assignments are not completed on time.

- Do you think Mike is being a good friend to Daniel?
- What do you think Daniel should do in this situation?
- What would you do in this situation?

Activity: Managing time

1   The correct term for something you do in preference to starting a particular task is a 'displacement activity'. In the workplace this includes things like often going to the water cooler to get a drink, and constantly checking emails and so on online. People who work from home may tidy up, watch television or even cook a meal to put off starting a job.

Write down *your* top three displacement activities.

2 Today is Wednesday. Sajid has several jobs to do tonight and has started well by making a 'to do' list. He's worried that he won't get through all the things on his list, and because he works on Thursday and Friday evenings that the rest will have to wait until Saturday.

a) Look through Sajid's list and decide which jobs are top priority and *must* be done tonight and which can be left until Saturday if he runs out of time.

b) Sajid is finding that his job is starting to interfere with his ability to do his assignments. What solutions can you suggest to help him?

Jobs to do

– File handouts from today's classes

– Phone Tom (left early today) to tell him the time of our presentation tomorrow has been changed to 11 am

– Research information online for next Tuesday's lesson

– Complete table from rough notes in class today

– Rewrite section of leaflet to talk about at tutorial tomorrow

– Write out class's ideas for the charity of the year, ready for course representatives meeting tomorrow lunchtime

– Redo handout Tom and I are giving out at presentation

– Plan how best to schedule assignment received today – deadline 3 weeks

– Download booklet from website ready for next Monday's class

Getting the most from work experience

On some BTEC First courses, all learners have to do a **work placement**. On others, they are recommended but not essential, or are required only for some optional units. If you are doing one, you need to prepare for it so that you get the most out of it. The checklists in this section will help.

Before you go checklist

1   Find out about the organisation by researching online.

2   Check that you have all the information you'll need about the placement.

3   Check the route you will need to take and how long it will take you. Always allow longer on the first day.

4   Check with your tutor what clothes are suitable and make sure you look the part.

5   Check that you know any rules or guidelines you must follow.

6   Check that you know what to do if you have a serious problem during the placement, such as being too ill to go to work.

7   Talk to your tutor if you have any special personal concerns.

8   Read the unit(s) that relate to your placement carefully. Highlight points you need to remember or refer to regularly.

9   Read the assessment criteria that relate to the unit(s) and use these to make a list of the information and evidence you'll need to obtain.

10 Your tutor will give you an official logbook or diary – or just use a notebook. Make notes each evening while things are fresh in your mind, and keep them safely.

While you're on work placement

Ideally, on your first day you'll be told about the company and what you'll be expected to do. You may even be allocated to one particular member of staff who will be your 'mentor'. However, not all firms operate like this, and if everyone is very busy, your **induction** may be rushed. If so, stay positive and watch other people to see what they're doing. Then offer to help where you can.

TRY THIS

You're on work experience. The placement is interesting and related to the job you want to do. However, you've been watching people most of the time and want to get more involved. Identify three jobs you think you could offer to do.

While you're there

1. Arrive with a positive attitude, knowing that you are going to do your best and get the most out of your time there.

2. Although you may be nervous at first, don't let that stop you from smiling at people, saying 'hello' and telling them your name.

3. Arrive punctually – or even early – every day. If you're delayed for any reason, phone and explain. Then get there as soon as you can.

4. If you take your mobile phone, switch it off when you arrive.

5. If you have nothing to do, offer to help someone who is busy or ask if you can watch someone who is doing a job that interests you.

6. Always remember to thank people who give you information, show you something or agree that you can observe them.

7. If you're asked to do something and don't understand what to do, ask for it to be repeated. If it's complicated, write it down.

8. If a task is difficult, start it and then check back that you are doing it correctly before you go any further.

9. Obey all company rules, such as regulations and procedures relating to health and safety and using machinery, the use of IT equipment and access to confidential information.

10. Don't rush off as fast as you can at the end of the day. Check first with your mentor or supervisor whether you can leave.

Coping with problems

Problems are rare but can happen. The most common ones are being bored because you're not given any work to do or upset because you feel someone is treating you unfairly. Normally, the best first step is to talk to your mentor at work or your supervisor. However, if you're very worried or upset, you may prefer to get in touch with your tutor instead – do it promptly.

TOP TIPS

Observing people who are skilled at what they do helps you learn a lot, and may even be part of your **assignment brief.**

Getting experience of work in sport

Work experience is not a mandatory unit on the BTEC First in Sport. However, your tutor may include Unit 13: Work Experience in Sport as an optional unit. If you do get the option to go on work experience, it can be a really good chance for you to explore a career that you are interested in. It will help you find out more about what you think may be your perfect job.

To get the most from work experience, you need to have a good think about what career you really want to pursue. The time you spend on work experience can help you in the future. Potential new employers will value good feedback from work experience supervisors. So you may find that your time spent on work experience could actually help land your dream job!

Activity: Selecting the perfect job for you

Draw a mind map to take show the types of things you might be looking for in your perfect job. Some factors to consider include:

- salary
- type of work
- working hours
- ability to use your qualifications (those you have and those you plan to get in the future)
- opportunity to demonstrate personal skills.

For example, this could be the start of a perfect job mind map.

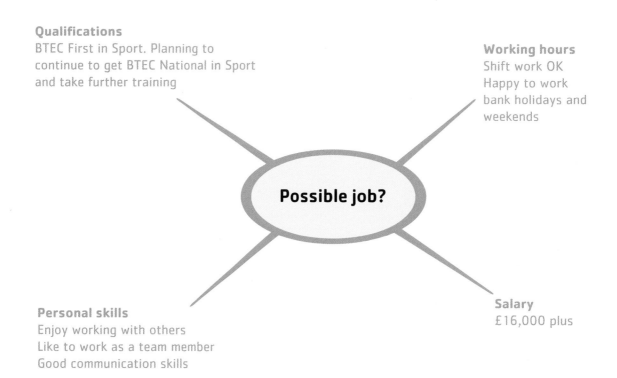

Qualifications
BTEC First in Sport. Planning to continue to get BTEC National in Sport and take further training

Working hours
Shift work OK
Happy to work bank holidays and weekends

Possible job?

Personal skills
Enjoy working with others
Like to work as a team member
Good communication skills

Salary
£16,000 plus

Now construct your own mind map.

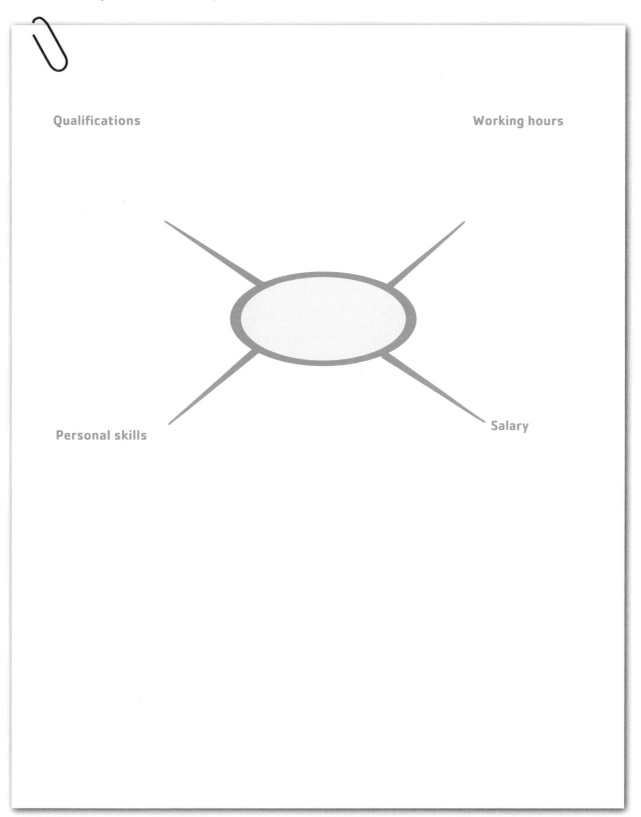

Qualifications

Working hours

Personal skills

Salary

Case study: Eleanor Smithson, on a work placement as a leisure centre assistant

What do you like best about the BTEC First in Sport?

I really enjoy PE lessons and have always found human biology really interesting. On this course, I get to have two days a week of lessons pretty much on both of these subjects. It is really great the way we can do some activities in PE, and then take the information we have gained and study this in the theory lessons.

Tell us about your work placement, and why you chose this option.

I am working in my local leisure centre as a leisure centre assistant. There are lots of reasons why I applied to the centre. It is only a 10 minute walk from my home. I go to the centre at least twice a week to play badminton and swim, so I thought it would be great to work there too. I don't mind the idea of working evenings and weekends, and I know you can do some training on the job. I really enjoy sport, so I would like to work in an area where I have easy access to sports facilities. I may even consider coaching or gym instructing in the future.

What did you like best about your work placement?

After a few days of settling in, I have been given more responsibility. I set up and take down the badminton nets. I get to shadow the lifeguards, and I watch them carry out the tests to check the chlorine levels of the pool. I stayed late one night to watch the lifeguard training. This was all about how to resuscitate a person who has nearly drowned, which was really interesting. I work shifts too, which is good, so although I sometimes start work early, on these days I get to go home at 2 pm and have the rest of the day to chill out.

What did you like least about your work placement?

Getting up for the early shift was not much fun – I had to be at the leisure centre for 6 am. I also don't really enjoy the cleaning part of the shift, which we have to do at the start and the end of the day. Helping with the cleaning duties can be a bit boring.

How do you record your progress on your work placement?

Our tutor has given us a diary to fill in every day. We write what we have done, and record the skills that we are developing.

Has the placement helped you decide if you want a job in a leisure centre?

Definitely! My supervisor is very pleased with my work and he has asked if I would be interested in applying for some part-time work next year when I am 16 years old. I will certainly be applying for this work.

Activity: Thinking about a work placement

1 What sort of work placement would you like to take part in?

2 What do you think would be best about this placement?

3 Which do you think would be the worst things about this placement?

4 Do you already have an idea of an organisation where you could carry out this work placement?

5 If so, how would you travel to this organisation?

Working with other people

Everyone finds it easy to work with people they like and far harder with those they don't. On your course you'll often be expected to work as a team to do a task. This gives you practice in working with different people.

You will be expected to:

- contribute to the task
- listen to other people's views
- adapt to other people's ways of working
- take responsibility for your own contribution
- agree the best way to resolve any problems.

These are quite complex skills. It helps if you understand the benefits to be gained by working cooperatively with other people and know the best way to achieve this.

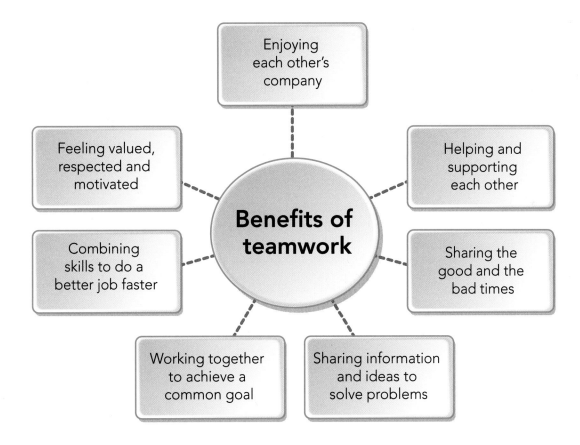

The benefits of good working relationships and teamwork

Golden rules for everyone (including the team leader!)

The secret of a successful team is that everyone works together. The role of the team leader is to make this as easy as possible by listening to people's views and coordinating everyone's efforts. A team leader is not there to give orders.

Positive teamwork checklist

✔ Be loyal to your team, including the team leader.

✔ Be reliable and dependable at all times.

✔ Be polite. Remember to say 'please' and 'thank you'.

✔ Think before you speak.

✔ Treat everyone the same.

✔ Make allowances for individual personalities. Give people 'space' if they need it, but be ready to offer support if they ask for it.

✔ Admit mistakes and apologise if you've done something wrong – learn from it but don't dwell on it.

✔ Give praise when it's due, give help when you can, and thank people who help you.

✔ Keep confidences, and any promises that you make.

 Do you:

a) shrug and say nothing in case he gets upset

b) ask why he didn't text you to give you warning

c) say that it's the last time you'll ever go anywhere with him and walk off?

Which do you think would be the most effective – and why?

Case study: Gary's work placement

Gary has been in his work placement at a leisure centre for one week. However, he is not getting on very well with the rest of his team, and his supervisor is clearly not happy with him.

Gary catches the bus to work, but he has found that they don't always come on time. When he travels during rush hour the journey to work takes 45 minutes, rather than the usual 20 minutes when it is not rush hour.

Gary has not had much experience of setting up sports equipment, such as badminton nets and five-a-side football goals, so he tries to avoid this aspect of his job. This means that other members of the team have to set up the equipment by themselves, which makes the job much longer.

Gary has never done any courses in customer care, and he does not know how to react when customers have a complaint.

Activity: Advising Gary

Read the case study about Gary carefully. What do you think Gary should do in order to help him to improve his relationship with the rest of his team and make his supervisor happy with his work? Consider the three areas that are identified as problems in the case study.

a) Time-keeping

b) Setting up equipment

c) Handling complaints

Activity: A good team member

Being a member of a team means that several people will be relying on you and, likewise, you will rely on the other members of the team too. In order to work well as a team, you all need to 'do your bit'.

Make a list of 10 rules that all team members should try to follow. Write alongside the rule why you think it is important, and describe the problems that might arise if team members do not stick to the rule.

1

2

3

4

5

6

7

8

9

10

Most people on a BTEC First in Sport course choose the course because they enjoy taking part in sports. Many sports are played as part of a team, and in order to get the most out of sport a person has to be able to work well as a member of a team.

Outdoor pursuit activities also require good teamworking skills. In rock climbing, for example, climbers will belay their partners on a climb. Good teamwork skills are essential to ensure the health and safety of the climbers.

There are many benefits to be gained from working as a team.

Activity: Teamwork in the sports industry

Teamwork is also essential in many jobs in the sports industry. Most careers in sport require people to work as part of a team and, perhaps, eventually to become a team leader. Test your knowledge about teamwork by completing these tasks.

1 As a person working in the sports industry, explain how you think you would be expected to work as a member of a team in these situations.

- Setting up a volleyball court.

- Cleaning the changing rooms.

- Checking the gym equipment at the end of the day.

- Getting the safety equipment ready for a walking expedition.

- Assisting a person who has been injured.

- Dealing with a customer complaint.

2 Working in the sports industry, you usually need to be able to work well as part of a team. Try to imagine (and describe) how these situations could affect you and your team.

○ You arrive 30 minutes late for your afternoon shift as a lifeguard.

○ You've finished cleaning your area of the sports centre, so you go to help a colleague finish cleaning his section of the centre.

○ You go out to lunch and get delayed on the way back. This means you end up taking an extra 15 minutes for your lunch break.

○ You finish your afternoon break early as a colleague asks you to help set up a volleyball court.

Getting the most from special events

BTEC First courses usually include several practical activities and special events. These enable you to find out information, develop your skills and knowledge in new situations and enjoy new experiences. They may include visits to external venues, visits from specialist speakers, and team events.

A visit to a museum is a great way to find out more about the topics you are studying.

Most learners enjoy the chance to do something different. You'll probably look forward to some events more than others. If you're ready to get actively involved, you'll usually gain the most benefit. It also helps to make a few preparations!

A visit from a sports practitioner

As part of your course, you may well have the opportunity to visit exhibitions and attend events that will help increase your understanding of the subject area. You may also have talks by experts in the subjects that you are studying.

How do you think you should behave when a visiting speaker comes to your school or college? Why is this?

How will you make notes from the speaker's talk?

How will you find out about the speaker before they come to deliver a talk?

What sort of questions do you plan to ask the speaker?

Case study: A trip to the Body Worlds exhibition

Body Worlds is an exhibition of the anatomy of humans. The bodies displayed have had their skin removed so that you can see their muscles. Some bodies are placed in sporting poses; one is placed in a pose to make it look like the body is kicking a football.

How has your trip helped you on your course?

The obvious subjects that it has helped me with are anatomy and physiology! It's one thing to see pictures and diagrams of muscles in a textbook, but it is so much clearer and more interesting seeing the real thing. I tried to identify different muscles on the bodies that I was seeing. I found that seeing the different poses really did make me think about how the body moves.

Did everyone on the trip enjoy the exhibition?

I think a few of my class were a bit shy at the beginning, but once they got over the initial unease, I think they all enjoyed it. Towards the end of the visit, we were going up really close to the exhibits to have a really good look at the different parts of the body.

How did you apply the knowledge gained from this exhibition?

I felt very confident in my anatomy and physiology assignment, particularly with my knowledge of the muscular system. I could also apply information gained from this visit to other units on the course, such as those which examine healthy lifestyles.

Special events checklist

✔ Check you understand how the event relates to your course.

✔ If a visit or trip is not something you would normally find very interesting, try to keep an open mind. You might get a surprise!

✔ Find out what you're expected to do, and any rules or guidelines you must follow, including about your clothes or appearance.

✔ Always allow enough time to arrive five minutes early, and make sure you're never late.

✔ On an external visit, make notes on what you see and hear. This is essential if you have to write about it afterwards, use your information to answer questions in an assignment, or do something practical.

✔ If an external speaker is going to talk to your class, prepare a list of questions in advance. Nominate someone to thank the speaker afterwards. If you want to record the talk, it's polite to ask first.

✔ For a team event, you may be involved in planning and helping to allocate different team roles. You'll be expected to participate positively in any discussions, to talk for some (but not all) of the time, and perhaps to volunteer for some jobs yourself.

✔ Write up any notes you make as soon as you can – while you can still understand what you wrote!

TRY THIS

At the last minute, you're asked to propose a vote of thanks to a visiting speaker on behalf of your class. What would you say?

Resources and research

Understanding resources

Resources are items that help you do something. The most obvious one is money! To obtain your BTEC First award, however, your resources are rather different.

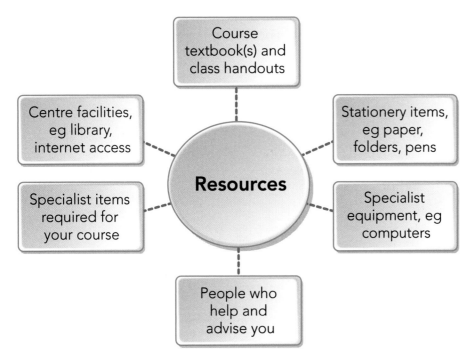

Different kinds of resources

Physical resources

Physical resources are things like textbooks, computers and any specialist equipment.
- Popular textbooks, laptops for home use and specialist equipment may need to be booked. Leaving it until the last minute is risky.
- You can ask for help if you don't know how to use resources properly.
- You should check what stationery and equipment you need at the start of your course and make sure you have it.
- You need to look after your resources carefully. This saves money and time spent replacing lost items.

People as resources

There are many people who can help you through your course:
- family members who help and support you
- your tutor

- friends in your group who collect handouts for you and phone you to keep you up to date when you're absent
- librarians and computer technicians, at your centre or your local library
- expert practitioners.

Expert practitioners

Expert practitioners have worked hard to be successful in their chosen area. They know the skills and knowledge needed to do the job properly. They can be invaluable when you're researching information. You can also learn a lot by watching them at work, especially if you can ask them questions about what they do, what they find hard and any difficulties they've had.

You need to be an expert to work with and advise others.

Try to observe more than one expert practitioner:
- It gives you a better picture about what they do.
- No single job will cover all aspects of work that might apply to your studies.
- You may find some experts more approachable and easy to understand than others. For example, if someone is impatient because they're busy it may be difficult to ask them questions, or if someone works very quickly you may find it hard to follow what they're doing.

If you have problems, just note what you've learned and compare it with your other observations. And there's always the chance that you're observing someone who's not very good at their job! You'll only know this for certain if you've seen what people should be doing.

Create your own resource list

You will use many different resources to help your studies into sport. These will include textbooks, internet sites, journals and CD-ROMS.

Go to your school or college library, and visit the 'sport' section. Spend some time looking at the different types of resources available.

Try to produce a list of useful:

- textbooks
- websites
- journals.

Make a note of the name of each resource and write a brief description of what it contains. Record this information in the table below, or make a similar version that you can store electronically on a computer.

This list will provide a starting point to help you when you have an assignment. You will know some resources that you can use to start your research. You should look to add to this list throughout the course. Try to use different sources of information in your work, rather than keep drawing on a small number of the same references for each assignment.

Textbook name	Author	Description

Website address	Description of content

Journal name	Description of content

Finding the information you need

The information explosion

There are lots of different ways to find out information – books, newspapers, magazines, TV, radio, CDs, DVDs, the internet. And you can exchange information with other people by texting, sending an email or phoning someone.

All this makes it much easier to obtain information. If you know what you're doing, you can probably find most of what you need sitting at a computer. But there are some dangers:

- Finding exactly what you want online takes skill. You need to know what you're doing.
- It's easy to get too much information and become overwhelmed.
- It's unlikely that everything you need will be available online.
- The information you read may be out of date.
- The information may be neither reliable nor true.

> Define what you are trying to find. (The more precise you are, the more likely you are to find what you're looking for.)

> Know where to look for it. (Remember: the internet is not the only source of information.)

> Recognise when you have found appropriate information.

> Know what to do with information once you've found it. (Make sure that you understand it, interpret it correctly and record the source where you found it.)

> Know when to stop looking (especially if you have a deadline).

Finding and using information effectively

Before you start

There are four things that will help you look in the right place and target your search properly.

Ask yourself ...	Because ...	Example
Exactly what do I need to find out?	It will save you time and effort.	If you need information about accidents, you need to know what type of accident and over what time period.
Why do I need this information and who is going to read it?	This puts the task into context. You need to identify the best type of information to obtain and how to get it.	If you're making a poster or leaflet for children, you'll need simple information that can be presented in a graphical format. If, however, you're giving a workplace presentation on accidents, you'll need tables and graphs to illustrate your talk.
Where can I find it?	You need to consider whether your source is trustworthy and up to date. The internet is great, but you must check that the sites you use are reliable.	To find out about accidents in the workplace you could talk to the health and safety at work officer. To find examples of accidents in your local area you could look through back copies of your local newspaper in the local library or newspaper offices.
What is my deadline?	You know how long you have to find the information and use it.	

TRY THIS

Schedule your research time by calculating backwards from the deadline date. Split the time you have 50/50 between searching for information and using it. This stops you searching for too long and getting lots of interesting material, but then not having the time to use it properly!

Your three main sources of information are:
- libraries or learning resource centres
- the internet
- asking other people, for example through interviews and questionnaires.

Researching in libraries

You can use the learning resource centre in your school or college, or a local public library. Public libraries usually have a large reference section with many resources available for loan, including CD-ROMs, encyclopaedias, government statistics, magazines, journals and newspapers, and databases such as Infotrac, which contains articles from newspapers and magazines over the last five years.

The librarian will show you how to find the resources you need and how to look up a specific book (or author) to check if it is available or is out on loan.

Some books and resources can only be used in the library itself, while others can be taken out on short-term or long-term loan. You need to plan how to access and use the resources that are popular or restricted.

Using your library

✔ If your centre has an intranet you might be able to check which books and CD-ROMs are available without actually visiting the library.

✔ All libraries have photocopying facilities, so take enough change with you to copy articles that you can't remove. Write down the source of any article you photocopy, ie the name and the date of the publication.

✔ Learn how to keep a reference file (or bibliography) in which you store the details of all your sources and references. A bibliography must include CDs, DVDs and other information formats, not just books and magazines.

✔ If your search is complicated, go at a quiet time when the librarian can help you.

✔ Don't get carried away if you find several books that contain the information you need. Too many can be confusing.

✔ Use the index to find information quickly by searching for key words. Scan the index using several likely alternatives.

✔ Only use books that you find easy to understand. A book is only helpful if you can retell the information in your own words.

Researching online

A good search engine such as Google will help you find useful websites. They look for sites based on the information you enter in the search box. In some cases, such as Ask.co.uk, you may get the chance to refine your choice after entering your key words or question.

Finding information on a website

Wikipedia is a popular free online encyclopaedia. It has been criticised because entries may be inaccurate as members of the public can edit the site. However, Wikipedia is trying to prevent this by organising professional editing.

If you're not sure whether something you read is correct, or if there is anything strange about it, check it against information on another site. Make sure you ask your tutor's opinion, too.

With large websites, it can be difficult to find what you need. Always read the whole screen – there may be several menus in different parts of the screen.

To help you search, many large websites have:

- their own search facility or a site map that lists site content with links to the different pages

- links to similar sites where you might find more information. Clicking a link should open a new window, so you'll still be connected to the original site.

TRY THIS

Search engines don't just find websites. On Google, the options at the top of your screen include 'images', 'news' and 'maps'. If you click on 'more' and then 'even more', you'll find other options, too. You'll usually find the most relevant information if you use the UK version of a search engine. Only search the whole web if you deliberately want to include European and American information.

To see this in action, go to www.pearsonhotlinks.co.uk, insert the express code 5681S and click on the link for this page.

There may be useful information and links at the top, foot or either side of a web page.

There are several other useful sites you could visit when researching online.

- **Directory sites** show websites in specific categories so you can focus your search at the start.
- **Forums** are sites, or areas of a website, where people post comments on an issue. They can be useful if you want to find out opinions on a topic. You can usually read them without registering.
- **News sites** include the BBC website as well as the sites for all the daily newspapers. Check the website of your local newspaper, too.

Printing information

- Only print information that you're sure will be useful. It's easy to print too much and find yourself drowning in paper.
- Make quick notes on your print-outs so that you remember why you wanted them. It will jog your memory when you're sorting through them later.
- If there's a printer-friendly option, use it. It will give you a print-out without unnecessary graphics or adverts.
- Check the bottom line of your print-outs. It should show the URL for that page of the website, and the date. You need those if you have to list your sources or if you want to quote from the page.

TRY THIS

To see how directory sites work go to www.pearsonhotlinks.co.uk, insert the express code 5681S and click on the link for this page.

TOP TIPS

Bookmark sites you use regularly by adding the URL to your browser. How to do this will depend on which browser you use, eg Internet Explorer, Firefox.

Researching by asking other people

You're likely to do this for two reasons:

- you need help from someone who knows a lot about a topic
- you need to find out several people's opinions on something.

Information from an expert

Explain politely why you are carrying out the investigation. Ask questions slowly and clearly about what they do and how they do it. If they don't mind, you could take written notes so you remember what they tell you. Put the name and title of the person, and the date, at the top. This is especially important if you might be seeing more than one person, to avoid getting your notes muddled up.

Ask whether you may contact them again, in case there's anything you need to check. Write down their phone number or email address. Above all, remember to say 'thank you'!

Case study: Information from a guest speaker

Leroy is studying for a BTEC First in Sport. He has always used the course textbook to help him with his assignment research. However, the school has occasional outside speakers that deliver presentations to his class. Leroy is a keen rugby player and hopes one day to become a rugby professional, so he is particularly interested when a former professional rugby player talks to the group about the lifestyle of an elite sports performer.

At the end of the presentation, Leroy asks several questions, receiving some very interesting and informative answers. These answers really help Leroy to understand one of the assignment tasks that he has been given. He uses these answers in his assignment, quoting the former rugby player as the source of the information. For this assignment, Leroy receives the highest grade that he has been awarded to date!

If you do not get the opportunity to talk to experts to find out information, you can try going on internet sites that have forums for learners to 'talk' to each other and to exchange ideas. Of course, you can always talk to your tutor/teacher.

TOP TIP

The internet and other data sources are great, but with so much information available how do you get to the important stuff? You need a research plan!

The opinions of several people

The easiest way to do this is with a questionnaire. You can either give people the questionnaire to complete themselves, or interview them and complete it yourself. Professional interviewers often telephone people to ask questions, but at this stage it's not a good idea unless you know the people you're phoning and they're happy for you to do this.

Devising a questionnaire

1 Make sure it has a title and clear instructions.

2 Rather than ask for opinions, give people options, eg yes/no, maybe/always, never/sometimes. This will make it easier to analyse the results.

3 Or you can ask interviewees to give a score, say out of 5, making it clear what each number represents, eg 5 = excellent, 3 = very good.

4 Keep your questionnaire short so that your interviewees don't lose interest. Between 10 and 15 questions is probably about right, as long as that's enough to find out all you need.

5 Remember to add 'thank you' at the end.

6 Decide upon the representative sample of people you will approach. These are the people whose views are the most relevant to the topic you're investigating.

7 Decide how many responses you need to get a valid answer. This means that the answer is representative of the wider population. For example, if you want views on food in your canteen, it's pointless only asking five people. You might pick the only five people who detest (or love) the food it serves.

Carrying out a questionnaire is an easy way of finding out what different people think of a certain issue or topic.

Managing your information

Whether you've found lots of information or only a little, assessing what you have and using it wisely is very important. This section will help you avoid the main pitfalls.

Organising and selecting your information

Organising your information

The first step is to organise your information so that it's easy to use.

- Make sure your written notes are neat and have a clear heading – it's often useful to date them, too.
- Note useful pages in any books or magazines you have borrowed.
- Highlight relevant parts of any handouts or leaflets.
- Work out the results of any questionnaires you've used.

Selecting your information

Re-read the **assignment brief** or instructions you were given to remind yourself of the exact wording of the question(s) and divide your information into three groups:

1. Information that is totally relevant.
2. Information that is not as good, but could come in useful.
3. Information that doesn't match the questions or assignment brief very much but that you kept because you couldn't find anything better!

Check there are no obvious gaps in your information against the questions or assignment brief. If there are, make a note of them so that you know exactly what you still have to find. Although it's ideal to have everything you need before you start work, don't delay if you're short of time.

Putting your information in order

Putting your information in a logical order means you can find what you want easily. It will save you time in the long run. This is doubly important if you have lots of information and will be doing the work over several sessions.

Case study: Developing a filing system

Alicia enjoys her BTEC First in Sport, but she finds she collects lots of information for each unit that she studies. She used to just put all her class notes into a folder at the end of each lesson. If she was working on the computer, she would just save any work in a folder called 'BTEC Sport'.

After the first term, Alicia found she could never find what she was looking for. Her folder was all jumbled up – there was work from different units all over the place. Her computer file was also very disorganised, so she would have to waste time opening up many different files before she eventually found the right one.

Alicia found herself getting into a panic over the situation. She chatted to her brother Charlie about the problem. Charlie worked for a leisure centre for a few months. He explained that the centre filed membership applications electronically. Every file is labelled with the applicant's second name, followed by the applicant's first name and date of application. It is really clear which file belongs to which member, and it is really easy to find a member's records.

Alicia now labels all her assignment files with the full assignment title and date. She finds that she is never confused about where her computer work has been saved. This feels so good that she has also developed her own paper filing system, and her paper notes are no longer disorganised. She can quickly refer to a piece of work or find some information she needs whenever necessary.

Organising your work

For your BTEC in Sport course, you will come across new and exciting information about sport and the sports industry. To help you study and to tackle your assignments, you will need to organise this information.

It is a good idea to buy yourself an A4 file with a ring binder. This can be used to hold A4 paper – if it is suitably hole punched – or material in A4 poly pockets.

Buy or make file dividers for this file, so that you can divide the material into separate units. For example, if you are studying the BTEC Level 2 Certificate in Sport, you will need three dividers because you will be taking three units. Label each divider with the name of the unit:

- Unit 1: Fitness Testing and Training
- Unit 2: Practical Sport
- Unit 3: Outdoor and Adventurous Activities

Place all your work from your lessons into the appropriate section.

Organising your assignments

Your tutor may organise files for you to keep your assignments in. If this is not the case, it would be a good idea to buy a second A4 file for your assignments. This is often referred to as a 'portfolio'. Again, buy dividers for each unit of the course that you are taking, and then place each assignment into the appropriate unit. This file must be kept in a very safe place as it will contain all the evidence that you will put together to pass the qualification.

Organising electronic work

If you produce your work on a computer, it is a good idea to keep your assignments in appropriately named folders on your system – for example, one might be named 'Practical sport', another 'Preparation for sport' etc. Whenever you are working on an assignment, you should always back up your work. Save it to both your hard drive and also an external source, such as a USB memory stick.

Interpreting and presenting your information

The next stage is to use your information to prepare the document and/or oral presentation you have to give. There are four steps:

1 Understand what you're reading.

2 Interpret what you're reading.

3 Know the best form in which to produce the information, bearing in mind the purpose for which it is required.

4 Create the required document so that it's in a suitable layout with correct spelling and punctuation.

Understanding what you read

As a general rule, never use information that you don't understand. However, nobody understands complex or unfamiliar material the first time they read it, especially if they just scan through it quickly. Before you reject it, try this:

Read it once to get the main idea.	Read it again, slowly, to try to take in more detail.	Look up any words you don't know in a dictionary to find out what they mean.
Write your own version.	Summarise the main points in your own words.	Read it a third time and underline or highlight the main points. (If this is a book or magazine that you shouldn't write in, take a photocopy first and write on that.)

Special note: Show both the article and your own version to your tutor to check your understanding. This will help you identify any points you missed out and help you improve your skills of interpreting and summarising.

Understanding unfamiliar information

Interpreting what you read

Interpreting what you read is different from understanding it. This is because you can't always take it for granted that something you read means what it says. The writer may have had a very strong or biased opinion, or may have exaggerated for effect. This doesn't mean that you can't use the information.

Strong opinions and bias

People often have strong points of view about certain topics. This may be based on reliable facts, but not always! We can all jump to conclusions that may not be very logical, especially if we feel strongly about something.

Things aren't always what they seem to be. Are these boys fighting or are they having a good time?

Exaggeration

Many newspapers exaggerate facts to startle and attract their readers.

LOCAL FIRM DOUBLES STAFF IN TWO WEEKS!

This newspaper headline sounds very positive. You could easily think it means employment is growing and there are more jobs in your area. Then you read on, and find the firm had only four staff and now has eight!

Tables and graphs

You need to be able to interpret what the figures mean, especially when you look at differences between columns or rows. For example, your friend might have an impressive spreadsheet that lists his income and expenditure. In reality, it doesn't tell you much until you add the figures up and subtract one from the other. Only then can you say whether he is getting into debt. And even if he is, you need to see his budget over a few months, rather than just one which may be exceptional.

Choosing a format

You may have been given specific instructions about the format and layout of a document you have to produce, in which case life is easy as long as you follow them! If not, think carefully about the best way to set out your information so that it is clear.

Different formats	Example
text	when you write in paragraphs or prepare a report or summary
graphical	a diagram, graph or chart
pictorial	a drawing, photograph, cartoon or pictogram
tabular	numerical information in a table

The best method(s) will depend on the information you have, the source(s) of your material and the purpose of the document – a leaflet for schoolchildren needs graphics and pictures to make it lively, whereas a report to company shareholders would be mainly in text form with just one or two graphs.

Stating your sources

Whatever format you use, if you are including other people's views, comments or opinions, or copying a table or diagram from another publication, you must state the source by including the name of the author, publication or the web address. This can be in the text or as part of a list at the end. Failure to do this (so you are really pretending other people's work is your own) is known as **plagiarism**. It is a serious offence with penalties to match.

Text format

Creating written documents gets easier with practice. These points should help.

Golden rules for written documents

1 Think about who will be reading it, then write in an appropriate language and style.

2 Ensure it is technically correct, ie no wrong spellings or bad punctuation.

3 Take time to make it look good, with clear headings, consistent spacing and plenty of white space.

4 Write in paragraphs, each with a different theme. Leave a line space between each one.

5 If you have a lot of separate points to mention, use bullets or numbered points. Numbered points show a certain order or quantity (step 1, step 2 etc). Use bullet points when there is no suggested order.

6 Only use words that you understand the meaning of, or it might look as if you don't know what you mean.

7 Structure your document so that it has a beginning, middle and end.

8 Prepare a draft and ask your tutor to confirm you are on the right track and are using your information in the best way.

Graphical format

TRY THIS ➡

Someone asks for directions to your house. Would you write a list or draw a diagram? Which would be easier for you and for the other person – and why?

Most people find graphics better than a long description for creating a quick picture in the viewer's mind. There are several types of graphical format, and you can easily produce any of these if you have good ICT skills.

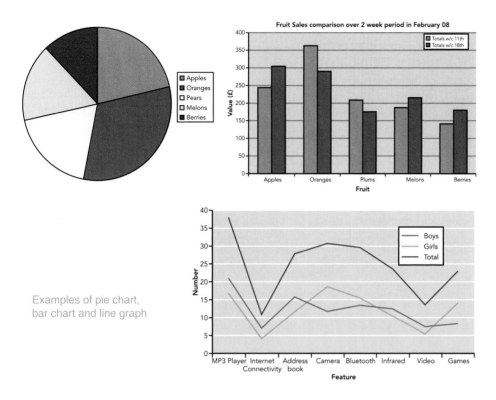

Examples of pie chart,
bar chart and line graph

Pictorial format

Newspapers and magazines use pictures to illustrate situations and reduce
the amount of words needed. It doesn't always have to be photographs
though. For example, a new building may be sketched to show what it will
look like.

A pictogram or pictograph is another type of pictorial format, such as charts
which use the image of an object (fruit, coins, even pizzas) to represent data,
such as the number eaten or amount spent.

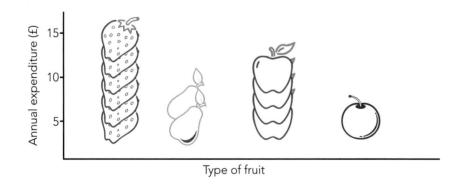

Tabular format

A table can be an easy way to communicate information. Imagine a retailer
preparing information about the items in stock. Text would be difficult to
understand and comparisons between stock levels and sales would be
almost impossible to make. A table, however, would easily show the fastest-
selling items.

Tables are also ideal if you are showing rankings – such as best-selling music or books.

Bestsellers list – September 2009

Position	Title	Author	Imprint	Publication
1 (New)	Lost Symbol, The	Brown, Dan	Bantam Press	15-Sep-2009
2 (1)	Complaints, The	Rankin, Ian	Orion	03-Sep-2009
3 (New)	Return Journey, The	Binchy, Maeve	Orion	17-Sep-2009
4 (7)	Sapphire	Price, Katie	Century	30-Jul-2009
5 (9)	Wolf Hall	Mantel, Hilary	Fourth Estate	30-Apr-2009
6 (3)	Week in December, A	Faulks, Sebastian	Hutchinson	03-Sep-2009
7 (2)	Alex Cross's Trial	Patterson, James	Century	10-Sep-2009
8 (4)	White Queen, The	Gregory, Philippa	Simon & Schuster Ltd	18-Aug-2009
9 (5)	Even Money	Francis, Dick & Francis, Felix	Michael Joseph	03-Sep-2009
10 (8)	206 Bones	Reichs, Kathy	William Heinemann	27-Aug-2009

National newspaper circulation – September 2009

	August 2009	August 2008	% change on last year	August 09 (without bulks)	March 2009 – August 2009	% change on last year
Sun	3,128,501	3,148,792	-0.64	3,128,501	3,052,480	-2.25
Daily Mail	2,171,686	2,258,843	-3.86	2,044,079	2,178,462	-4.45
Daily Mirror	1,324,883	1,455,270	-8.96	1,324,883	1,331,108	9.44
Daily Star	886,814	751,494	18.01	886,814	855,511	16.65
The Daily Telegraph	814,087	860,298	-5.37	722,644	807,328	-6.73
Daily Express	730,234	748,664	-2.46	730,234	727,824	-1.32
Times	576,185	612,779	-5.97	529,746	588,471	-4.63
Financial Times	395,845	417,570	-5.2	365,269	411,098	-6.7
Daily Record	347,302	390,197	-10.99	345,277	350,306	-10.59
Guardian	311,387	332,587	-6.37	311,387	332,790	-4.11
Independent	187,837	230,033	-18.34	148,551	198,445	-16.76

Activity: Interpreting and presenting information

There are many different ways to present information that you have gathered from your research. Some research may be data that shows the performance of a team or an individual. Other information may concern techniques, such as the required skills needed to serve an ace in tennis.

In sport, data often shows how well one team has performed compared to another. In its simplest form, this is what is recorded in football results:

Manchester Utd 2 Chelsea 1

Liverpool 0 Arsenal 3

Results are also presented in a table format to show the performance over a season (or over a season to date). Find out the scores for a sports league of your choice and then record the results of the leading teams by completing the table on the next page.

Name of team	Matches played	Points

You will also be dealing with other types of data on your course, such as heart rate at rest and heart rate during exercise. The table below presents data that shows how one person's heart rate changed during a 10-minute exercise period. The first record (for 0 minutes) shows the heart rate was at rest when the person was at rest.

Time spent exercising (minutes)	Heart rate (beats per minute)
0	60
1	65
2	84
3	85
4	90
5	91
6	95
7	99
8	100
9	102
10	105

Plot this information on a graph. The axes of the graph are drawn for you below.

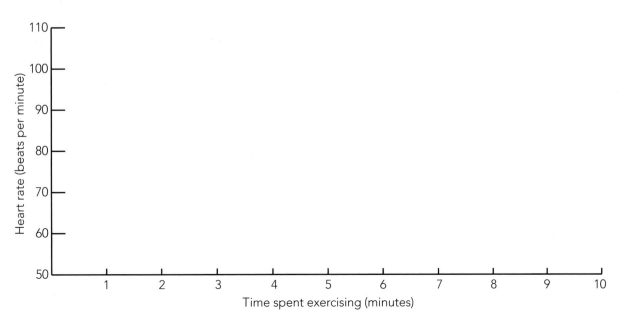

Now interpret the results. Look at your graph and at the data in the table.

1 Which format do you think best shows this person's heart rate changes while taking part in exercise: the table format or the graph?

2 Explain your answer to question 1. Why do you think that the format you have chosen is better.

3 What happened to the person's heart rate once they started exercising? Why was this?

4 From the changes in heart rate shown by this data, name three different types of sport or exercise that you think this person may have been taking part in. Explain each of your choices.

i

ii

iii

Keeping a logbook

You will probably be taking part in some form of practical sport during your course. A really good way to track your progress is to keep a logbook. A logbook is really a diary in which you can track which skills you have learned, record your performance, and set targets for the future.

An example of a suitable logbook format for sport is shown below. Fill in the logbook page for a sport of your choice.

Name	
Date	
Course	
Sport	

Identify the skills required to play your sport:

List the dates you acquired or learned skills and techniques to assist your development in your sports (such as passing, footwork, attacking, defending, spatial awareness, timing etc). Record areas for improvement in each case.

Date	Skill	Areas for improvement

After each game (or session) of your selected sport, use this table to evaluate your own performance. Again identify your strengths and areas for improvement.

Date	Skills	Tactics	Techniques	Strengths	Areas for improvement

Making presentations

Presentations help you to learn communication skills.

Some people hate the idea of standing up to speak in front of an audience. This is quite normal, and you can use the extra energy from nerves to improve your performance.

Presentations aren't some form of torture devised by your tutor! They are included in your course because they help you learn many skills, such as speaking in public and preparing visual aids. They also help you practise working as a team member and give you a practical reason for researching information. And it can be far more enjoyable to talk about what you've found out rather than write about it!

There's a knack to preparing and giving a presentation so that you use your energies well, don't waste time, don't fall out with everyone around you, and keep your stress levels as low as possible. Think about the task in three stages: preparation, organisation and delivery.

Preparation

Start your initial preparations as soon as you can. Putting them off will only cause problems later. Discuss the task in your team so that everyone is clear about what has to be done and how long you have to do it in.

Divide any research fairly among the team, allowing for people's strengths and weaknesses. You'll also need to agree:
- which visual aids would be best
- which handouts you need and who should prepare them
- where and when the presentation will be held, and what you should wear
- what questions you might be asked, both individually and as a team, and how you should prepare for them.

Once you've decided all this, carry out the tasks you've been allocated to the best of your ability and by the deadline agreed.

TOP TIPS

Keep visual aids simple but effective and check any handouts carefully before you make lots of copies.

Organisation

This is about the planning you need to do as a team so that everything will run smoothly on the day.

Delivery

This refers to your performance during the presentation. Being well prepared and well organised helps stop you panicking. If you're very nervous at the start, take a few deep breaths and concentrate on the task, not yourself. It's quite normal to be nervous at the start but this usually fades once you get under way. You might even enjoy it …

Top tips for delivering a good presentation

✔ Rehearse, rehearse, rehearse!

✔ Write notes on flash cards to remind you of key things that you need to say.

✔ Practise looking up from your cards when you are talking.

✔ Time yourself to see if your presentation lasts for the time allocated.

✔ Include illustrations and slides, if possible, to engage the audience.

✔ Practise saying any complicated words again and again so that they don't cause any problems in your actual presentation.

✔ Make sure you understand what you are saying – you may have questions on your presentation at the end.

What else do you think you could do to help you prepare for a presentation?

1

2

3

4

5

Activity: Presenting information on sports techniques

Where techniques need to be taught, it is often better to show a person demonstrating the technique. You can use video clips or pictures to show where the body position should be and how the sports equipment should be used.

Think about these different types of information. Then explain what you think is the best way to present the information:

1 The results from your school league netball team.

2 How to perform a lay up in basketball.

3 How a player's breathing rate changes from rest and then over the next 20 minutes while taking part in a game of rugby.

4 The runs scored every 5 overs in a one-day cricket international.

Overs	5	10	15	20	25	30	35	40	45	50
Runs	12	58	69	85	125	198	210	242	263	292

5 The technique required to perform a 'Fosbury flop' in the high jump event.

Case study: Learner quotes about making presentations

Most people start off feeling uncomfortable about talking in front of a group of people, whether you know them or not. This is what some real learners have said about having to give presentations as part of their BTEC course.

"I actually feel more comfortable giving a presentation rather than having to write an essay. What I really enjoy about it is the fact that sometimes we have to prepare a presentation as a whole group. I like that we work together to find information and then we take turns presenting different points. The fact that I am not the only one out there and I am part of a supportive team makes it fun for me."

Gabriela, 16, BTEC Level 2 First in Performing Arts

"Although presentations are very stressful, when I present my work it helps to hang my ideas together and I find I can express what I want to say more clearly than when I write things down. Instant feedback is helpful and boosts my confidence for the next time."

Ethan, 19, BTEC Level 2 First in Creative Media Production

"I think presentations are useful but I find them difficult to deliver – relying heavily on my memory, which is very nerve-wracking. We were told that presentation would be part of our assessment. I really worried about it and couldn't sleep the night before – stressing out about what I was going to say. I hated the first few minutes, but after that I was OK."

Will, 16, BTEC Level 2 First in Engineering

"I was very nervous about presenting to my class until I took part in the Young Enterprise scheme and had to present the results of our project to over 200 people including the mayor! After that presenting to my class mates didn't feel too nerve-wracking at all."

Lizzy, 17, BTEC Level 2 First in Business

"I used to dread presentations on my course, but found that if I went through my notes again and again until I knew the presentation inside out, it made it much easier and the presentations generally went well."

Javinder, 17, BTEC Level 3 National in Construction

"I used to hate presenting to other people on my course, until I realised that most of them were as nervous about it as I was!"

Koichi, 21, BTEC Level 3 National in Art and Design

"Less is more! I used to rely on props and as I was nervous about forgetting things or running out of things to say I talked far too quickly. I had to repeat everything as nobody knew what I was on about! Some of my best presentations have been done without using slides or any other props at all, just talking (slowly of course) to my audience."

Laura, 18, BTEC Level 3 National in Health & Social Care

"I used to be petrified of talking in front of other people but over time I've learned that, if I prepare well before a presentation, I usually feel much more confident on the day. If I know my material, I don't have to look down at my notes all the time and can make eye contact with the audience. Taking a few deep breaths before I begin keeps me calm and allows me to focus."

Katie, 19, BTEC Level 3 National in Creative Media Production

"I prefer to be assessed by oral presentations as I'm dyslexic and my written work lets me down all the time. Everyone tells me that I really shine and show that I know my stuff when I present it to the rest of the group."

Sam, 17, BTEC Level 3 National in Business

Your assessments

The importance of assignments

All learners on BTEC First courses are assessed by means of **assignments**. Each one is designed to link to specific **learning outcomes** and **grading criteria**. At the end of the course, your assignment grades put together determine your overall grade.

To get the best grade you can, you need to know the golden rules that apply to all assignments, then how to interpret the specific instructions.

10 golden rules for assignments

1. Check that you understand the instructions.

2. Check whether you have to do all the work on your own, or if you will do some as a member of a group. If you work as a team, you need to identify which parts are your own contributions.

3. Always write down any verbal instructions you are given.

4. Check the final deadline and any penalties for not meeting it.

5. Make sure you know what to do if you have a serious personal problem, eg illness, and need an official extension.

6. Copying someone else's work (**plagiarism**) is a serious offence and is easy for experienced tutors to spot. It's never worth the risk.

7. Schedule enough time for finding out the information and doing initial planning.

8. Allow plenty of time between talking to your tutor about your plans, preparations and drafts, and the final deadline.

9. Don't panic if the assignment seems long or complicated. Break it down into small, manageable chunks.

10. If you suddenly get stuck, ask your tutor to talk things through with you.

Case study: A presentation on nutrition

Stephen has been given an assignment that requires him to deliver a presentation on nutrition in sport. He really enjoys the subject, but he has never given a presentation before. He is very nervous at the prospect of delivering the presentation but sets about his work. He spends a lot of time carrying out research to make sure that he has the information he needs to put it into a presentation format.

Stephen has learned how to use PowerPoint. He decides that he will present his work using this software. He selects the key points for each part of his presentation and writes them on to PowerPoint slides. He also adds in pictures to illustrate his work.

Once the PowerPoint presentation is ready, Stephen makes notes on flash cards to remind himself what to say with each slide. He then has a go at delivering his presentation in his bedroom. After 45 minutes practising, he times himself to check that the full presentation is the right length (between 5 and 8 minutes). He then practises the presentation in front of his mum, which helps him to get used to speaking in front of an audience.

Later, when it comes to delivering his presentation in front of his tutor, Stephen is only a little nervous. He has spent so long preparing and practising for the assignment that he is confident it will go well. The tutor asks him a few questions when he finishes, and Stephen is pleased that he is able to answer each question.

Stephen comes away with a distinction grade for his work. He now feels much more relaxed at the prospect of delivering another presentation.

Interpreting the instructions

Most assignments start with a **command word** – describe, explain, evaluate etc. These words relate to how complex the answer should be.

Command words

Learners often don't do their best because they read the command words but don't understand exactly what they have to do. These tables show you what is required for each grade when you see a particular command word.

Command words and obtaining a pass

Complete ...	Complete a form, diagram or drawing.
Demonstrate ...	Show that you can do a particular activity.
Describe ...	Give a clear, straightforward description that includes all the main points.
Identify ...	Give all the basic facts relating to a certain topic.
List ...	Write a list of the main items (not sentences).
Name ...	State the proper terms related to a drawing or diagram.
Outline ...	Give all the main points, but without going into too much detail.
State ...	Point out or list the main features.

Examples:

- **List** the main features on your mobile phone.
- **Describe** the best way to greet a customer.
- **Outline** the procedures you follow to keep your computer system secure.

Command words and obtaining a merit

Analyse ...	Identify the factors that apply, and state how these are linked and how each of them relates to the topic.
Comment on ...	Give your own opinions or views.
Compare ... Contrast ...	Identify the main factors relating to two or more items and point out the similarities and differences.
Competently use ...	Take full account of information and feedback you have obtained to review or improve an activity.
Demonstrate ...	Prove you can carry out a more complex activity.
Describe ...	Give a full description, including details of all the relevant features.
Explain ...	Give logical reasons to support your views.
Justify ...	Give reasons for the points you are making so that the reader knows what you're thinking.
Suggest ...	Give your own ideas or thoughts.

Examples:
- **Explain** why mobile phones are so popular.
- **Describe** the needs of four different types of customer.
- **Suggest** the type of procedures your employer would need to introduce to keep the IT system secure.

Command words and obtaining a distinction

Analyse ...	Identify several relevant factors, show how they are linked, and explain the importance of each.
Compare ... Contrast ...	Identify the main factors in two or more situations, then explain the similarities and differences, and in some cases say which is best and why.
Demonstrate ...	Prove that you can carry out a complex activity, taking into account information you have obtained or received to adapt your original idea.
Describe ...	Give a comprehensive description which tells a story to the reader and shows that you can apply your knowledge and information correctly.
Evaluate ...	Bring together all your information and make a judgement on the importance or success of something.
Explain ...	Provide full details and reasons to support the arguments you are making.
Justify ...	Give full reasons or evidence to support your opinion.
Recommend ...	Weigh up all the evidence to come to a conclusion, with reasons, about what would be best.

Examples:
- **Evaluate** the features and performance of your mobile phone.
- **Analyse** the role of customer service in contributing to an organisation's success.
- **Justify** the main features on the website of a large, successful organisation of your choice.

TRY THIS

Check the command word you are likely to see for each of your units in the **grading grid** in advance. This tells you the **grading criteria** for the unit so that you know the evidence you will have to present.

TOP TIPS

Think of assignments as an opportunity to demonstrate what you've learned and to get useful feedback on your work.

Getting the best result

Ask your tutor for a copy of the specification for one of the units that you are studying. Any unit will do because they are all presented in the same format. Have a look through the different sections.

- The learning outcomes state exactly what you should know, understand and be able to do when you have finished the unit.
- The unit content is the subject-specific material that you will be studying.
- The grading grid tells you what you have to present as evidence for assessment.
- There are three grading criteria: pass, merit and distinction.

Now read through the headings under the greyed-out section of the grading criteria grid. What does it say about achieving pass, merit or distinction grade? Write a brief explanation here:

Pass

Merit

Distinction

You must achieve all the pass criteria to be awarded the pass grade. You must achieve all the pass criteria and all the merit criteria to be awarded the merit grade, and you must achieve all the grading criteria to be awarded the distinction grade.

Suppose it is the end of the year, and your tutor is signing off a portfolio using a tracking sheet. This table shows a learner's performance for Unit 1: Fitness Testing and Training.

Grading criterion	P1	P2	P3	P4	P5	P6	M1	M2	M3	D1	D2
Achieved	✔	✔	✔	✔	✔	✔	✔		✔	✔	✔

This learner would be awarded a pass grade. The learner cannot be awarded a merit because M2 has not been achieved, and cannot be awarded distinction because, although the learner has achieved all the distinction criteria, he hasn't achieved all the grading criteria.

The grading grids use several key words and phrases. Make sure that you know what they mean.

Word/phrase	What it means
Interpret	
Analyse	
Describe	
Explain	
Evaluate	
Carry out	

With the exception of the mathematics unit, the word 'evaluate' is only ever used in the merit and distinction criteria. Use a dictionary to find a general definition for the word.

Evaluate: _____

Sample assignment

Note about assignments
All learners are different and will approach their assignment in different ways.
The sample assignment that follows shows how one learner answered a brief to achieve pass, merit and distinction level criteria. The learner work shows just one way in which grading criteria can be evidenced. There are no standard or set answers. If you produce the required evidence for each task then you will achieve the grading criteria covered by the assignment.

Front sheet

Make sure the front sheet is completed appropriately, including your full name, the title of your qualification, the unit number and the unit name in full.

Make sure you have your work ready to hand in on, or before, the completion date. This is the assignment deadline date set by your centre. It is also a very good idea to ask your tutor to look through the work before you hand it in and provide feedback as to how you can improve the work.

Enter here the actual date you are submitting (handing in) your work, which should be on, or before, the completion date. Your centre may have specific guidelines for handing in work, so make sure you know what these are before submitting the work.

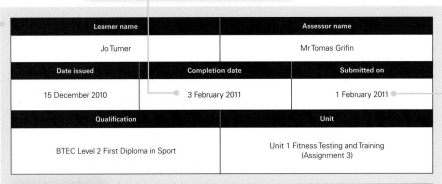

Learner name		Assessor name
Jo Turner		Mr Tomas Grifin

Date issued	Completion date	Submitted on
15 December 2010	3 February 2011	1 February 2011

Qualification	Unit
BTEC Level 2 First Diploma in Sport	Unit 1 Fitness Testing and Training (Assignment 3)

Assignment title	Assessing Fitness Levels – How Fit are You?

In this assessment you will have opportunities to provide evidence against the following criteria.
Indicate the page numbers where the evidence can be found.

Criteria reference	To achieve the criteria the evidence must show that the student is able to:	Task no.	Page numbers
P4	Carry out four different fitness tests for different components of fitness, recording the results accurately	1	Pages 1–5
P5	Interpret their test results and personal level of fitness	2	Page 6
M2	Explain their test results and personal level of fitness, identifying strengths and areas for improvement	3	Pages 7–8
D1	Evaluate their test results and personal level of fitness, considering the level required to achieve excellence in a selected sport	3	Pages 7–8

Learner declaration

I certify that the work submitted for this assignment is my own and research sources are fully acknowledged.

Learner signature: *Jo Turner*   Date: *1 February 2011*

The evidence you produce needs to meet the unit assessment and grading criteria which are listed in this section on the assignment front sheet.

Your signature confirms that you completed the work and that it has not been copied from other sources such as a textbook, internet site or another student.

This section indicates to your teacher/tutor where they can find the work that you have produced for each criteria. Some sections may meet more than one criterion: make sure this is clearly shown in this section.

Assignment brief

The scenario allows you to relate assignment tasks to the real world of sporting professions.

You should always keep the assignment title in mind so that you keep focused on the main theme of the assignment.

Unit title	Unit 1 Fitness Testing and Training
Qualification	BTEC Level 2 First Diploma in Sport
Start date	15 December 2010
Deadline date	3 February 2011
Assessor	Mr Grifin

Assignment title	Assessing Fitness Levels – How Fit are You?

The purpose of this assignment is to:
Enable learners to investigate their personal fitness levels by participating in a series of fitness tests and interpreting test results.

Scenario
You have recently joined a local sports club, and the coach wants to assess your fitness levels in order to design a training programme. You have been asked to participate in four different fitness tests for different components of fitness.

Task 1
Carry out four different fitness tests for different components of fitness, providing an accurate written record of your results. You will need to ensure that you adhere to pre-test procedures, follow standard test procedures, and consider the reliability, validity and practicality of the tests.

This provides evidence for P4

Task 2
Provide a written interpretation of your test results and personal level of fitness. Use published data tables to compare your fitness test results to normative data and to the fitness levels required for excellence.

This provides evidence for P5

Task 3
You will need to provide a written explanation of your test results and personal level of fitness, identifying strengths and areas for improvement (M2). You will then need to provide a written evaluation of your test results and personal level of fitness, showing that you have considered the level required to achieve excellence in your chosen sport (D1).

This provides evidence for M2 and D1

Sources of information

Textbooks
Adams GM – *Exercise Physiology Laboratory Manual: Health and Human Performance* (McGraw Hill Higher Education, 2001) ISBN: 9780072489125
Allen MB – *Sports Exercise and Fitness: A Guide to Reference and Information Sources* (Libraries Unlimited Inc, 2005) ISBN: 9781563088193
Buckley J, Holmes J, Mapp G – *Exercise on Prescription: Cardiovascular Activity for Health* (Butterworth-Heinemann, 1999) ISBN: 9780750632881
Dalgleish J, Dollery S – *The Health & Fitness Handbook* (Longman, 2001) ISBN: 9780582418790
Davis J – *Fitness for Games Players* (NCF, 1996) ISBN: 9780947850104
Franks BD, Howley ET – *Fitness Leader's Handbook* (Human Kinetics Europe, 1998) ISBN: 9780880116541
Fulcher K, Fox P – *Your Personal Trainer: The Ultimate Guide to Getting Fit for any Sport* (Metro Books, 2002) ISBN: 9781843580027
Harris B et al – *BTEC First Sport:* (Heinemann, 2006) ISBN: 9780748783915
Hazeldine R – *Fitness for Sport* (The Crowood Press, 2000) ISBN: 9781861263360
Honeybourne J – *BTEC First in Sport* (Nelson Thornes, 2006) ISBN: 9780748783915
Moran GT, McGlynn G – *Cross Training for Sports: Programmes for 26 Sports* (Human Kinetics, 1997) 9780880114936
Scott A – *GCSE PE for Edexcel* (Heinemann, 2001) ISBN: 9780435506360
Sharkey BJ, Gaskill SE – *Fitness and Health* (Human Kinetics, 2006) ISBN: 9780736056144
Watson AWS – *Physical Fitness and Athletic Performance; A Guide for Students, Athletes and Coaches* (Longman, 1996) ISBN: 9780582091108

The evidence you produce can take many forms, including PowerPoint presentations, leaflets, posters, laboratory reports etc. The assignment brief will specify the evidence required, so always try to ensure that it is in this format.

The tasks state what you need to do to produce the assessment evidence to meet the unit assessment and grading criteria.

These textbooks and websites have been selected to enable you to find out more about fitness testing and training and find research materials that will help support your assignment work

Websites

Useful websites for this assignment include:

British Association of Sport and Exercise Sciences
www.bases.org.uk

Human Kinetics
www.humankinetics.com

Top End Sports
www.topendsports.com

Sport Science
www.sportsci.org

Sports Coach UK
www.sportscoachuk.org

American College of Sports Medicine
www.acsm.org

This brief has been verified as being fit for purpose.			
Assessor	Mr Grifin		
Signature	Tomas Grifin	Date	1 December 2010
Internal verifier	Mr J Churchill		
Signature	Jack Churchill	Date	1 December 2010

Sample learner work

Assessing Fitness Levels – How Fit are You?

Learner name: Jo Turner

Task 1 (P4) – Carry out fitness tests and record your results.

The four different fitness tests I've carried out for different components of fitness are:

1. Sit and Reach Test (for flexibility)

2. Multi-stage Fitness Test (for VO2 max – aerobic endurance)

3. Vertical Jump Test (for power)

4. Skinfold Testing (for percent body fat)

I have completed a data sheet for each test, showing my results. These are shown on the next four pages.

Make sure you use a suitable proforma to record your fitness testing results and use correct units for tests, as the learner has here.

Hope College of FE Form 1.0

Sit and Reach Test

Learner Name: Jo Turner   Date: 16.12.2010

Gender: Female

Wt = 58 kg

Ht = 1.61 m

Trial 1 = 18 cm
Trial 2 = 18 cm
Average = 18 cm

Re-test (same day)
Trial 1 = 18 cm
Trial 2 = 22 cm
Average = 20 cm

Units of measurement = cm

Notes: equipment – we used a standard sit and reach box.

It is good practice to show equipment used and data sources.

Sample learner work: page 3

Hope College of FE Form 2.0

Multi-stage Fitness Test

Learner Name: Jo Turner   Date: 17.12.2010

Gender: Female

Trial 1 Result: Level 6 Shuttle 8 = VO_2 max = 35.7 ml/kg/min

Learner Name: Jo Turner   Date: 10.01.2011

Trial 2 Result: Level 6 Shuttle 10 = VO_2 max = 36.4 ml/kg/min

Notes: we used a data table to look up our VO_2 max result (ml/kg/min) from the level and shuttle we got to. Equipment – multi-stage fitness test audiotape, tape recorder, 4 cones.

The learner has made sure information is clearly recorded in table format, including results from more than one test (if possible) for reliability.

Hope College of FE Form 3.0

Vertical Jump Test Data Sheet

Learner Name: Jo Turner   Date: 12.01.2011

Gender: Female
Weight in jump clothes = 58 kg

Ht = 1.61m

Reach position (closest cm) = 39

	Height jumped (cm)
Trial 1	68
Trial 2	70
Average	69

	Height jumped (cm)
Trial 1	65
Trial 2	69
Average	67

Difference between best average jump height and reach =
69 – 39 = 30 cm

Notes: Equipment used – a vertical jump board and gymnasts' chalk.
I used the Lewis Nomogram to work out my power result.

My Power Result = 73 kgm/s.

Working out has been shown to illustrate how the height has been measured. This is good practice. The learner used the Lewis nomogram to determine their anaerobic power result (kgm/s).

Assessment criterion P4 has been achieved – the learner has now carried out four different fitness tests for four different components of fitness, accurately recording their results.

Hope College of FE Form 4.0

Skinfold Testing

Learner Name: Jo Turner   Date: 20.01.2011

Gender: Female

Age: 16 years

Skinfold Site	Triceps (mm)	Thigh (mm)	Suprailium (mm)
Trial 1	9	23	11
Trial 2	9	24	11
Average	9	23.5	11

Results
Total Skinfolds = TRICEPS (mm) + THIGH (mm) + SUPRAILIUM (mm)
= 9 + 23.5 + 11
= 43.5 mm

I used the J-P Nomogram to get my percent body fat result = 17 % Body Fat.

Notes: I used the Jackson & Pollock skinfold method for females, which was Triceps, Thigh and Suprailium. We worked in small groups to practise the skinfold technique and to take the measurements. Boys in the class had to use different skinfold sites to the girls. Equipment: We used Harpenden and Slimguide skinfold calipers, a tape measure and a pen to mark the sites.

The learner has tabulated their overall results from the four different fitness tests, correctly interpreted results, and provided a clear indication of overall personal levels of fitness from each test. Assessment criterion P5 has been achieved.

Task 2 – Interpretation of My Overall Fitness Test Results (P5)

This table shows my overall fitness test results:

Fitness component	Fitness Test	Trial 1	Trial 2	Fitness Result	Units	Interpretation of Test Results (Rating)
Flexibility	Sit & Reach Test	18	20	20	cm	Excellent
Aerobic endurance (VO_2 max)	Multi-stage Fitness Test	35.7	36.4	36.4	ml/kg/min	Average
Power	Vertical Jump	73	73	73	kgm/s	Average
Body composition	Skinfold testing	17	17	17	% body fat	Slim

These results show that my flexibility is excellent (results table by Hueger, 1989). I did better on my second test than my first, I think I was feeling more warmed-up which helped my stretching ability. My multi-stage fitness test aerobic endurance fitness result was average. We did this test twice in the sports hall on different days and I got my highest result (36.4 ml/kg/min) on my second trial. We looked at data tables published by the Police Force to interpret our results. My aerobic fitness is classed as average for my age.

My power result from the vertical jump test was average (Shepherd, 2000). I got a result of 73 kgm/s. From the skinfold testing, my percent body fat result was 17% and according to data published by the Police Force, this means I am slim.

The learner has explained and evaluated their test results and personal levels of fitness, including details of what was done well and why, and also their areas for improvement and what can be done to help to improve these specified components of fitness. The learner has considered the levels required to achieve excellence in their sport. Grading Criteria M2 and D1 have been achieved.

Sample learner work: page 7

Task 3 – Explain (M2) and evaluate (D1) test results

I am pleased with my fitness test results, particularly with my flexibility test result which was classed as excellent (Hueger, 1989). This means that my trunk forward flexion, hamstring, hip and lower back range of motion is excellent for my age. This is a strength for me because my two hobbies are playing netball and dance (ballet and jazz), so I think this is how my flexibility has developed well. I need to make sure I remain supple and flexible, my dance classes help with this as we always start and finish with lots of stretches. At the end of dance class we do developmental stretching. Also, our netball coach always includes stretching exercises as part of our warm-up and cool-down in training sessions, so I think flexibility will always be a strength for me. It helps to have good flexibility for netball, I play GA and I'm not that tall, so need to jump and reach to receive balls in the circle. For the sit and reach test, anything over 20+ cm is classed as excellent, I got 20 cm and with regular flexibility training maybe I will be able to reach all the way to the end of the box!

For the multi-stage fitness test, my highest result was Level 6 Shuttle 10, giving me a VO_2 max of 36.4 ml/kg/min. I felt a bit sick when I finished, so I know I really pushed myself hard. From the Police Force data table, my result is only average for 15–19 year old females. I was a bit disappointed with this, but think it is correct because during netball matches I do get out of breath quite easily, so this is an area I definitely want to improve on. I could do Fartlek or interval training to improve my aerobic fitness, and this would help me during netball matches because I shouldn't get out of breath so quickly and my body will become more efficient which will help my performance. Elite female athletes aged 18–22 years can have a VO_2 max of 63 ml/kg/min and young world-class athletes can have a VO_2 max of at least 70 ml/kg/min. So, I have a lot of room for improvement with my VO_2 of 36.4 ml/kg/min.

My vertical jump anaerobic power result was 73 kgm/s, which is about average for my age, so the power of my quadriceps muscle group is average. I think I can improve on this, particularly by doing something like plyometric training. I could do a plyometrics circuit for netball, which would definitely help improve the anaerobic power of my quadriceps muscles and help improve my jumping ability in netball, which would be good. I would be aiming for a power result of above 90 kgm/s, which according to Shepherd (2000) is classed as above average for college-aged females.

My skinfold testing was a good result and a strength for me. My result was 17% body fat, which means I am slim according to the Police Force (aged 16–29 years) data tables. I don't need to do anything to improve here. The 'slim' category is 13–20%, so I just need to maintain my percent body fat in this category. Top netballers have a percent body fat which is about the same as mine and some have percent body fat in the acceptable category (21–25% body fat), so as long as I maintain my % fat at 17%, my body composition is fine for me to perform well in netball.

Remember to reference any sources you have used. This shows you have done your research and avoids plagiarism issues.

Sample learner work: page 8

Assignment References

Adams GM (1989); [Vertical Jumps of College Physical Education Majors]. Unpublished raw data.

Baun WB, Baun MR, Raven PB (1981); A Nomogram for the Estimate of Percent Body Fat from Generalised Equations. Research Quarterly for Exercise and Sport 52 (3): 284–380.

Hueger WWK (1989); Sit and Reach Test Tables. Lifetime Physical Fitness and Wellness. Morton Publishing.

Jackson AS, Pollock ML, Ward A (1980); Generalised Equations for Predicting Body Density of Women. Medicine and Science in Sports and Exercise, 12, 175–182.

Police Force Fitness Assessment Mark Sheet.

Sharkey BJ (1990); Physiology of Fitness. Human Kinetics, Champaign, Illinois.

Shepherd P (2000); [Vertical Jumps of College-Aged Physical Education Students]. Unpublished raw data.

Observation record

The observation record provides evidence to show that your assessor/tutor observed you carrying out the four different fitness tests. It needs to be signed by you and your assessor/tutor to confirm that these activities actually took place and confirm the assessment criterion achieved (P4).

Learner name	Jo Turner
Assessor name	Mr T. Grifin
Qualification	BTEC Level 2 First Diploma in Sport
Unit number and title	Unit 1: Fitness Testing and Training – Assignment 3 – Task 1

Description of activity undertaken (please be as specific as possible)

Carry out four different fitness tests for different components of fitness, recording the results accurately.
Fitness tests conducted:
- Flexibility sit and reach test
- Multi-stage fitness test (aerobic endurance)
- Anaerobic power vertical jump test
- Skinfold testing (body composition – percent body fat)

Assessment and grading criteria

P4: Carry out four different fitness tests for different components of fitness, recording results accurately.
Assessment – Criterion P4 has been met.

How the activity meets the requirements of the assessment and grading criteria

Jo successfully carried out four different fitness tests as stated (below). A data collection results sheet was completed for each fitness test undertaken. For each test, Jo adhered to pre-test procedures including informed consent and calibration of equipment. Standard test protocol was followed for each test. Throughout test methodology Jo showed awareness of issues relating to validity, reliability and practicality of the tests undertaken and how these could affect results obtained. Results were recorded in a valid and accurate manner throughout.
- Flexibility sit and reach test (16.12.2010)
- Multi-stage fitness test (aerobic endurance) (17.12.2010)
- Anaerobic power vertical jump test (12.01.2011)
- Skinfold testing (body composition – percent body fat) (20.01.2011)

Learner signature	Jo Turner	Date	20 January 2011
Assessor signature	Mr T. Grifin	Date	20 January 2011

Assessor's comments

This section shows if you have achieved each of the criteria – 'Y' is yes and 'N' is no.

Qualification	BTEC Level 2 First Diploma in Sport	Year	2010–2011
Unit number and title	Unit 1: Fitness Testing and Training	Learner name	Jo Turner

Grading criteria	Achieved?
P4 carry out four different fitness tests for different components of fitness, recording the results accurately	Y
P5 interpret their test results and personal level of fitness	Y
M2 explain their test results and personal level of fitness, identifying strengths and areas for improvement	Y
D1 evaluate their test results and personal level of fitness, considering the level required to achieve excellence in a selected sport	Y

Learner feedback

I enjoyed this assignment, because there was lots of practical and it was fun carrying out the fitness tests. I found it very interesting to find out what my fitness levels are like and compare them to other people in my group and also to published data tables.

Assessor feedback

This is an excellent piece of work Jo. You have successfully carried out four different fitness tests for different components of fitness and interpreted your test results and personal level of fitness. Throughout the practical testing you worked methodically and recorded results accurately. You have successfully met criteria P4 and P5. Results have been explained and sufficiently evaluated, including identifying your strengths and areas for improvement and considering the level required for excellence. Evidence provided is sufficient to meet grading criteria M2 and D1. Your work shows evidence of additional research and you have made a great effort with referencing sources of information to help interpret data results. Keep up the good work!

Action plan

Continue to read generally around the subject and build on your excellent work. Remember to include references in text where appropriate (as well as in your overall references section); this is good practice, particularly when using published data to interpret your results.

Assessor signature	Tomas Grifin	Date	10 February 2011
Learner signature	Jo Turner	Date	15 February 2011

Detailing what you enjoyed and also any problems that you had will help you in future assignments. It may also help your tutor when they come to revise the assignment, and this could help future learners.

The action plan shows you what you need to do in the future to help you with either the assignment that has just been assessed or future assignments. It is an important tool in improving your work.

Coping with problems

Most learners sail through their BTEC First with no major problems. Unfortunately, not everyone is so lucky. Some may have personal difficulties or other issues that disrupt their work so they are late handing in their assignments. If this happens to you, it's vital to know what to do. This checklist should help.

Checklist for coping with problems

✔ Check that you know who to talk to.

✔ Don't sit on a problem and worry about it. Talk to someone promptly, in confidence. It's always easier to cope if you've shared it with someone.

✔ Most centres have professional counsellors you can talk to if you prefer. They won't repeat anything you say to them without your permission.

✔ If you've done something wrong or silly, people will respect you more if you are honest, admit where you went wrong and apologise promptly.

TOP TIPS

If you have a serious complaint or concern, talk to your chosen tutor first – for example, if you believe an assignment grade is unfair. All centres have official procedures to cover important issues such as appeals about assignments and formal complaints, but it's usually sensible to try to resolve a problem informally first.

Case study: Coping with problems

Dan is a 16-year-old student and he has nearly completed his BTEC First Diploma in Sport. A year ago, he was having lots of problems with the course and, at that time, it didn't look like he was going to finish the course.

What sort of problems were you having?

Looking back I think my main problem was with time management. I found the course really interesting, but I just couldn't cope with the amount of coursework that we were given. We had been given an assignment timetable so I knew when to expect the work, but I just didn't put the time aside to get the work done.

What happened next?

As the assignments started to get handed out, I still went out in the evenings or watched television instead of making a start on the work. Each assignment had about a two-week time frame to get the work done, but I just started to work the night before it was due in. I then found that one night was not nearly long enough to do the research and answer the tasks. It also meant I couldn't speak to my tutor to get some help with anything that I didn't understand. This meant that I didn't hand work in on time, and also that the work I did hand in was not as good as it could have been. Eventually, I had so many assignments that I had not finished, some for which the deadline had passed and others that were due in very soon, that I really didn't know where to start.

How did your tutor help you?

My tutor knew that I was struggling, so we had a chat about what was going wrong. I told my tutor that I had so much work to do, that I did not know where to start. She then helped me to devise an action plan that really helped me to get back on track. The plan listed all the assignments that I had to do. It was like a diary of what I needed to do and when I had to do it. For example, on Monday, straight after school I had to do the research for my fitness testing assignment, and then on Tuesday I would plan to answer the task from that assignment. This planned out my work for the next three weeks to a point where I would be up to date.

Did you stick to your action plan?

Yes, most of the time. The action plan allowed for one 'day off' a week, when I could relax and forget about work for the day. On the odd evening where I didn't complete all the work on my action plan, I caught up on my day off.

What advice would you give to others?

I would definitely say that you should start an assignment on the day you get it. Most tutors are happy to take assignments in early, so if you finish before the deadline, hand them in. By starting the assignment as soon as you get it, you have time to speak to a tutor if you are having any problems. Tutors can help you to understand the tasks, give you ideas on where to look for help, and put you on the right track.

Activity: Dealing with problems completing assignments

Here is one of the grading criteria from Unit 1: Fitness Testing and Training

P6 describe the effects of psychological factors on sports training and performance

Your tutor gives you two weeks to complete an assignment task that addresses grading criterion P6. She asks you to hand in a portfolio of evidence.

Some problems that you might come across as you carry out the assignment are listed below. State one strategy that you might use to overcome each problem.

1 You are unclear about what evidence the portfolio should contain.

2 You leave it too late before starting to write up the assignment.

3 You can't find the information that you need to complete the task.

4 Writing is not one of your strongest points.

Skills building

To do your best in your assignments you need a number of skills, including:

- your **personal, learning and thinking skills**
- your **functional skills** of ICT, mathematics and English
- your proofreading and document-production skills.

Personal, learning and thinking skills (PLTS)

These are the skills, personal qualities and behaviour that you find in people who are effective and confident at work. These people enjoy carrying out a wide range of tasks, always try to do their best, and work well alone or with others. They enjoy a challenge and use new experiences to learn and develop.

Activity: How good are your PLTS?

1 Do this quiz to help you identify areas for improvement.

  a) I get on well with other people.

    Always   **Usually**   **Seldom**   **Never**

  b) I try to find out other people's suggestions for solving problems that puzzle me.

    Always   **Usually**   **Seldom**   **Never**

  c) I plan carefully to make sure I meet my deadlines.

    Always   **Usually**   **Seldom**   **Never**

  d) If someone is being difficult, I think carefully before making a response.

    Always   **Usually**   **Seldom**   **Never**

  e) I don't mind sharing my possessions or my time.

    Always   **Usually**   **Seldom**   **Never**

  f) I take account of other people's views and opinions.

    Always   **Usually**   **Seldom**   **Never**

  g) I enjoy thinking of new ways of doing things.

    Always   **Usually**   **Seldom**   **Never**

  h) I like creating new and different things.

    Always   **Usually**   **Seldom**   **Never**

  i) I enjoy planning and finding ways of solving problems.

    Always   **Usually**   **Seldom**   **Never**

j) I enjoy getting feedback about my performance.

Always   Usually   Seldom   Never

k) I try to learn from constructive criticism so that I know what to improve.

Always   Usually   Seldom   Never

l) I enjoy new challenges.

Always   Usually   Seldom   Never

m) I am even-tempered.

Always   Usually   Seldom   Never

n) I am happy to make changes when necessary.

Always   Usually   Seldom   Never

o) I like helping other people.

Always   Usually   Seldom   Never

Score 3 points for each time you answered 'Always', 2 points for 'Usually', 1 point for 'Seldom' and 0 points for 'Never'. The higher your score, the higher your personal, learning and thinking skills.

2 How creative are you? Test yourself with this activity. Identify 50 different objects you could fit into a matchbox at the same time! As a start, three suitable items are a postage stamp, a grain of rice, a staple. Can you find 47 more?

BTEC FACTS

Your BTEC First qualification is at Level 2. Qualifications in functional skills start at Entry level and continue to Level 2. (You don't need to achieve functional skills to gain any BTEC qualification, and the evidence from a BTEC assignment can't be used towards the assessment of functional skills.)

Functional skills

Functional skills are the practical skills you need to function confidently, effectively and independently at work, when studying and in everyday life. They focus on the following areas:

- Information and Communications Technology (ICT)
- Maths
- English.

You may already be familiar with functional skills. Your BTEC First tutors will give you more information about how you will continue to develop these skills on your new course.

ICT skills

These will relate directly to how much 'hands-on' practice you have had on IT equipment. You may be an experienced IT user, and using word-processing, spreadsheet and presentation software may be second nature. Searching for information online may be something you do every day – in between downloading music, buying or selling on eBay and updating your Facebook profile!

Or you may prefer to avoid computer contact as much as possible. If so, there are two things you need to do:

1 Use every opportunity to improve your ICT skills so that you can start to live in the 21st century!

2 Make life easier by improving your basic proofreading and document preparation skills.

Proofreading and document preparation skills

Being able to produce well-displayed work quickly will make your life a lot easier. On any course there will be at least one unit that requires you to use good document preparation skills.

Tips to improve your document production skills

✔ If your keyboarding skills are poor, ask if there is a workshop you can join. Or your library or resource centre may have software you can use.

✔ Check that you know the format of documents you have to produce for assignments. It can help to have a 'model' version of each type in your folder for quick reference.

✔ Practise checking your work by reading word by word – and remember not to rely on spellcheckers (see page 56).

Activity: How good are your ICT skills?

1a) Test your current ICT abilities by responding *honestly* to each of the following statements.

i) I can create a copy of my timetable using a word-processing or spreadsheet package.
True   **False**

ii) I can devise and design a budget for myself for the next three months using a spreadsheet package.
True   **False**

iii) I can email a friend who has just got broadband to say how to minimise the danger of computer viruses, what a podcast is, and also explain the restrictions on music downloads.
True   **False**

iv) I can use presentation software to prepare a presentation containing four or five slides on a topic of my choice.
True   **False**

v) I can research online to compare the performance and prices of laptop computers and prepare an information sheet using word-processing software.
True   **False**

vi) I can prepare a poster, with graphics, for my mother's friend who is starting her own business preparing children's party food, and attach it to an email to her for approval.
True   **False**

TRY THIS

Learning to touch type can save you hours of time. To check your keyboarding skills go to www.pearsonhotlinks.co.uk, insert the express code 5681S and click on the link for this page.

TOP TIPS

Print your work on good paper and keep it flat so that it looks good when you hand it in.

1b) Select any one of the above to which you answered False and learn how to do it.

2 Compare the two tables below. The first is an original document; the second is a typed copy. Are they identical? Highlight any differences you find and check them with the key on page 95.

Name	Date	Time	Room
Abbott	16 July	9.30 am	214
Grey	10 August	10.15 am	160
Johnston	12 August	2.20 pm	208
Waverley	18 July	3.15 pm	180
Jackson	30 September	11.15 am	209
Gregory	31 August	4.20 pm	320
Marshall	10 September	9.30 am	170
Bradley	16 September	2.20 pm	210

Name	Date	Time	Room
Abbott	26 July	9.30 am	214
Gray	10 August	10.15 am	160
Johnson	12 August	2.20 pm	208
Waverley	18 July	3.15 am	180
Jackson	31 September	11.15 am	209
Gregory	31 August	4.20 pm	320
Marshall	10 September	9.30 pm	170
Bradley	16 August	2.20 pm	201

Maths or numeracy skills

Four easy ways to improve your numeracy skills

1 Work out simple calculations in your head, like adding up the prices of items you are buying. Then check if you are correct when you pay for them.

2 Set yourself numeracy problems based on your everyday life. For example, if you are on a journey that takes 35 minutes and you leave home at 11.10 am, what time will you arrive? If you are travelling at 40 miles an hour, how long will it take you to go 10 miles?

3 Treat yourself to a Maths Training program.

4 Check out online sites to improve your skills. Go to www.pearsonhotlinks.co.uk, insert the express code 5681S and click on the link for this page.

TOP TIPS

Quickly test answers. For example, if fuel costs 85p a litre and someone is buying 15 litres, estimate this at £1 x 15 (£15) and the answer should be just below this. So if your answer came out at £140, you'd immediately know you'd done something wrong!

Activity: How good are your maths skills?

Answer as many of the following questions as you can in 15 minutes. Check your answers with the key on page 95.

1   a) 12 + 28 = ?

   i) 30   ii) 34   iii) 38   iv) 40   v) 48

   b) 49 ÷ 7 = ?

   i) 6   ii) 7   iii) 8   iv) 9   v) 10

   c) ½ + 1¼ = ?

   i) ¾   ii) 1½   iii) 1¾   iv) 2¼   v) 3

   d) 4 × 12 = 8 × ?

   i) 5   ii) 6   iii) 7   iv) 8   v) 9

   e) 16.5 + 25.25 – ? = 13.25

   i) 28.5   ii) 31.25 iii) 34.5 iv) 41.65 v) 44

2   a) You buy four items at £1.99, two at 98p and three at £1.75. You hand over a £20 note. How much change will you get? _____

   b) What fraction of one litre is 250 ml? _____

   c) What percentage of £50 is £2.50? _____

   d) A designer travelling on business can claim 38.2p a mile in expenses. How much is she owed if she travels 625 miles? _____

   e) You are flying to New York in December. New York is five hours behind British time and the flight lasts eight hours. If you leave at 11.15 am, what time will you arrive? _____

   f) For your trip to the United States you need American dollars. You find that the exchange rate is $1.5 dollars.

   i)   How many dollars will you receive if you exchange £500? _____

   ii) Last year your friend visited New York when the exchange rate was $1.8. She also exchanged £500. Did she receive more dollars than you or fewer – and by how much? _____

   g) A security guard and his dog patrol the perimeter fence of a warehouse each evening. The building is 480 metres long and 300 metres wide and the fence is 80 metres out from the building on all sides. If the guard and his dog patrol the fence three times a night, how far will they walk? _____

English skills

Your English skills affect your ability to understand what you read, prepare a written document, say what you mean and understand other people. Even if you're doing a practical subject, there will always be times when you need to leave someone a note, tell them about a phone call, read or listen to instructions – or write a letter for a job application!

Six easy ways to improve your English skills

1. Read more. It increases the number of words you know and helps to make you familiar with correct spellings.

2. Look up words you don't understand in a dictionary and check their meaning. Then try to use them yourself to increase your vocabulary.

3. Do crosswords. These help increase your vocabulary and practise your spelling at the same time.

4. You can use websites to help you get to grips with English vocabulary, grammar and punctuation. Go to www.pearsonhotlinks.co.uk, insert the express code 5681S and click on the link for this page.

5. Welcome opportunities to practise speaking in class, in discussion groups and during presentations – rather than avoiding them!

6. Test your ability to listen to someone else by seeing how much you can remember when they've finished speaking.

Activity: How good are your English skills?

1 In the table below are 'wrong' versions of words often spelled incorrectly. Write the correct spellings on the right. Check your list against the answers on page 95.

Incorrect spelling	Correct spelling
accomodation	
seperate	
definate	
payed	
desparate	
acceptible	
competant	
succesful	

2 Correct the error(s) in these sentences.

a) The plug on the computer is lose.

b) The car was stationery outside the house.

c) Their going on they're holidays tomorrow.

d) The principle of the college is John Smith.

e) We are all going accept Tom.

3 Punctuate these sentences correctly.

a) Toms train was late on Monday and Tuesday.

b) She is going to France Belgium Spain and Italy in the summer.

c) He comes from Leeds and says its great there.

4 Read the article on copyright.

Copyright

Anyone who uses a photocopier can break copyright law if they carry out unrestricted photocopying of certain documents. This is because The Copyright, Designs and Patents Act 1988 protects the creator of an original work against having it copied without permission.

Legally, every time anyone writes a book, composes a song, makes a film or creates any other type of artistic work, this work is treated as their property (or copyright). If anyone else wishes to make use of it, they must get permission to do so and, on occasions, pay a fee.

Licences can be obtained to allow educational establishments to photocopy limited numbers of some publications. In addition, copies of an original document can be made for certain specific purposes. These include research and private study. Under the Act, too, if an article is summarised and quoted by anyone, then the author and title of the original work must be acknowledged.

a) Test your ability to understand unfamiliar information by responding to the following statements with 'True' or 'False'.

i) Students and tutors in schools and colleges can copy anything they want.
True   False

ii) The law which covers copyright is The Copyright, Designs and Patents Act 1988.
True   False

iii) A student photocopying a document in the library must have a licence.
True   False

iv) Copyright only relates to books in the library.
True   False

v) If you quote a newspaper report in an assignment, you don't need to state the source.
True   False

vii) Anyone is allowed to photocopy a page of a book for research purposes.
True   False

b) Make a list of key points in the article, then write a brief summary in your own words.

5 Nikki has read a newspaper report that a horse racing in the Kentucky Derby had to be put down. The filly collapsed and the vet couldn't save her. Nikki says it's the third time in two years a racehorse has had to be put down in the US. As a horse lover she is convinced racing should be banned in Britain and the US. She argues that fox hunting was banned to protect foxes, and that racehorses are more important and more expensive than foxes. Darren disagrees. He says the law is not working, hardly anyone has been prosecuted and fox hunting is going on just like before. Debbie says that animals aren't important whilst there is famine in the world.

a) Do you think the three arguments are logical? See if you can spot the flaws and check your ideas with the suggestions on page 95.

b) Sporting activities and support for sporting teams often provoke strong opinions. For a sport or team of your choice, identify two opposing views that might be held. Then decide how you would give a balanced view. Test your ideas with a friend or family member.

Answers

Skills building answers

ICT activities

2 Differences between the two tables are highlighted in bold.

Name	Date	Time	Room
Abbott	**16** July	9.30 am	214
Grey	10 August	10.15 am	160
Johnston	12 August	2.20 pm	208
Waverley	18 July	3.15 **pm**	180
Jackson	**30** September	11.15 am	209
Gregory	31 August	4.20 pm	320
Marshall	10 September	9.30 **am**	170
Bradley	16 **September**	2.20 pm	**210**

Maths/numeracy activities

1 **a)** iv, **b)** ii, **c)** iii, **d)** ii, **e)** i

2 **a)** £4.83, **b)** ¼, **c)** 5%, **d)** £238.75, **e)** 2.15 pm, **f) i)** $750 **ii)** $150 dollars more, **g)** 6.6 km.

English activities

1 Spellings: accommodation, separate, definite, paid, desperate, acceptable, competent, successful

2 Errors:
   a) The plug on the computer is <u>loose</u>.
   b) The car was <u>stationary</u> outside the house.
   c) <u>They're</u> going on <u>their</u> holidays tomorrow.
   d) The <u>principal</u> of the college is John Smith.
   e) We are all going <u>except</u> Tom.

3 Punctuation:
   a) Tom's train was late on Monday and Tuesday.
   b) She is going to France, Belgium, Spain and Italy in the summer.
   c) He comes from Leeds and says it's great there.

4 **a) i)** False, **ii)** True, **iii)** False, **iv)** False, **v)** False, **vi)** False, **vii)** True

5 A logical argument would be that if racehorses are frequently injured in a particular race, eg one with difficult jumps, then it should not be held. It is not logical to compare racehorses with foxes. The value of the animal is irrelevant if you are assessing cruelty. Darren's argument is entirely different and unrelated to Nikki's. Whether or not fox hunting legislation is effective or not has no bearing on the danger (or otherwise) to racehorses. Finally, famine is a separate issue altogether. You cannot logically 'rank' problems in the world to find a top one and ignore the others until this is solved!

Accessing website links

Links to various websites are referred to throughout this BTEC Level 2 First Study Skills Guide. In order to ensure that these links are up to date, that they work and that the sites aren't inadvertently linked to any material that could be considered offensive, we have made the links available on our website: www.pearsonhotlinks.co.uk. When you visit the site, please enter the express code 5681S to gain access to the website links and information on how they can be used to help you with your studies.

Useful terms

Apprenticeships

Schemes that enable you to work and earn money at the same time as you gain further qualifications (an NVQ award and a technical certificate) and improve your functional skills. Apprentices learn work-based skills relevant to their job role and their chosen industry. Go to www.pearsonhotlinks.co.uk, insert the express code 5681S and click on the link for this useful term to find out more.

Assessment methods

Methods, such as practical tasks and assignments, which are used to check that your work demonstrates the learning and understanding you need to obtain the qualification.

Assessor

The tutor who marks or assesses your work.

Assignment

A complete task or mini-**project** set to meet specific grading criteria.

Assignment brief

The information and instructions related to a particular assignment.

BTEC Level 3 Nationals

Qualifications you can take when you have successfully achieved a Level 2 qualification, such as BTEC First. They are offered in a variety of subjects.

Credit value

The number of credits attached to your BTEC course. The credit value increases relative to the length of time you need to complete the course, from 15 credits for a BTEC Certificate to 30 credits for a BTEC Extended Certificate and 60 credits for a BTEC Diploma.

Command word

The word in an assignment that tells you what you have to do to produce the type of answer that is required, eg 'list', 'describe', 'analyse'.

Educational Maintenance Award (EMA)

This is a means-tested award which provides eligible learners under 19, who are studying a full-time course at a centre, with a cash sum of money every week. Go to www.pearsonhotlinks.co.uk, insert the express code 5681S and click on the link for this useful term to find out more.

Functional skills

The practical skills that enable all learners to use and apply English, Maths and ICT both at work and in their everyday lives. They aren't compulsory to achieve on the course, but are of great use to you.

Grade

The rating of pass, merit or distinction that is given to an assignment you have completed, which identifies the standard you have achieved.

Grading criteria

The standard you have to demonstrate to obtain a particular grade in the unit. In other words, what you have to prove you can do.

Grading grid

The table in each unit of your BTEC qualification specification that sets out the grading criteria.

Indicative reading

Recommended books, magazines, journals and websites whose content is both suitable and relevant to the unit.

Induction

A short programme of events at the start of a course or work placement designed to give you essential information and introduce you to other people so that you can settle in easily.

Internal verification

The quality checks carried out by nominated tutors at all centres to ensure that all assignments are at the right level and cover appropriate learning outcomes. The checks also ensure that all **assessors** are marking work consistently and to the same standards.

Learning outcomes

The learning and skills you must demonstrate to show that you have learned a unit effectively.

Levels of study

The depth, breadth and complexity of knowledge, understanding and skills required to achieve a qualification determines its level. Level 2 is equivalent to GCSE level (grades A* to C). Level 3 equates to GCE A-level. As you successfully achieve one level, you can progress on to the next. BTEC qualifications are offered at Entry Level, then Levels 1, 2, 3, 4, 5, 6 and 7.

Mandatory units

On a BTEC Level 2 First course, these are the compulsory units that all learners must complete to gain the qualification.

Optional units

Units on your course from which you may be able to make a choice. They help you specialise your skills, knowledge and understanding, and may help progression into work or further education.

Personal, learning and thinking skills (PLTS)

The skills and qualities that improve your ability to work independently and be more effective and confident at work. Opportunities for developing these are a feature of all BTEC First courses. They aren't compulsory to achieve on the course, but are of great use to you.

Plagiarism

Copying someone else's work or work from any other sources (eg the internet) and passing it off as your own. It is strictly forbidden on all courses.

Portfolio

A collection of work compiled by a learner – for an **assessor** – usually as evidence of learning.

Project

A comprehensive piece of work which normally involves original research and planning and investigation either by an individual or a team. The outcome will vary depending upon the type of project undertaken. For example, it may result in the organisation of a specific event, a demonstration of a skill, a presentation, or a piece of writing.

Tutorial

An individual or small group meeting with your tutor at which you discuss the work you are currently doing and other more general course issues.

Unit content

Details about the topics covered by the unit and the knowledge and skills you need to complete it.

Work placement

Time spent on an employer's premises when you carry out work-based tasks as an employee and also learn about the enterprise to develop your skills and knowledge.

Work-related qualification

A qualification designed to help you to develop the knowledge and understanding you need for a particular area of work.